DALLAS
GOT IT
RIGHT!

Sam Wyly, Laurie Matthews, and Andrew Wyly

OnFire Books
Helping world changers share their story

Clovercroft Publishing

Dallas Got it Right!

Published by Clovercroft Publishing, Franklin, Tennessee in association with OnFire Marketing.

Edited by Tammy Kling and Tiarra Tompkins

Copy Edit by Adept Content Solutions

Cover and Interior Design by Suzanne Lawing

Printed in the United States of America

ISBN: 978-1-945507-75-5

INTRODUCTION

In the pages to follow, we share our love for Dallas and the historical significance of this great city and the surrounding areas with you. Dallas is known for having a great economy that survives booms and busts better than most, but it's so much more than that.

An article in *Forbes*, "Move Over, San Francisco: Dallas Tops Our List of The Best Cities for Jobs in 2017," noted that unlike San Francisco, Dallas has multiple points of economic strength (not just technology).

This book is about many communities and towns and is a combination of culture, people, business, arts, and family values. *Dallas Got It Right!* touches on many of the memorable and magnificent aspects of the small towns, neighborhoods, and people that have made Dallas and the surrounding cities and towns, what it is. It is not solely focused on Dallas proper because of the global impact the citizens have made. We live in a world connected by people, cultures, and commerce.

Many people have relocated to Texas from places like California and New York, Asia and Europe, citing reasons such as family, culture, and strong values. Several other individuals and companies moved for economic reasons.

This book, co-authored with my daughter, Laurie Matthews, and son, Andrew Wyly, counts the reasons Dallas feeds the world, outproduces the Middle East in oil and gas, and serves as an epicenter for business management, technology, and investment opportunities.

Each of my six children, the executive producers of this story, helped make this book great.

We tell stories with pictures because every picture tells a story.

Dallas Got It Right! is the tale of a lot of little towns with families and organizations and businesses that have created massive impact. We're calling it greater Dallas, because it goes far north beyond Frisco to Colorado Springs, east to Jackson,

Mississippi through Delhi and Louisiana Tech, and then south to Aggie Land, and west to White Sands.

It's an area rich in history and entrepreneurial in spirit, expansive in technology, and unbounded by city limits. Built on cotton, cows, oil, the military, computer technology, wholesaling, and retail, you'll remember, "Our Dallas feeds the world. Our Dallas is the technology capital of the world. Our Dallas is vital to America's military muscle."

We'll visit a Dallas that goes beyond Elm Street and Main Street (if you live here, you already know these popular areas), and we'll look at others full of vibrant neighborhoods and characters.

What's the future of Dallas' collection of towns and counties? This is an area that will continually shape entrepreneurs and their families, influence ideas and the arts, give back for generations, withstand recessions, and stand the test of time. It's a great place to live for those who were born here, and for everyone else who got here as fast as they could!

Enjoy this journey through the past and the future.

ALL ROADS LEAD TO DALLAS

Sam Wyly was raised in small-town Louisiana and got his MBA from the University of Michigan. His road to Dallas was via a plane ride from Monroe to Shreveport to Tyler, and finally to Love Field.

"A foolish consistency is the hobgoblin of little minds."
RALPH WALDO EMERSON

CONTENTS

THE EARLY YEARS

Dallas is, and always has been, an innovation economy. No state embodies the spirit of independence and entrepreneurship more than Texas, and no city better exemplifies the successful blend of historical reverence and future growth more than Dallas and the surrounding towns. The area was settled by tough pioneers, and it is the modern pioneers who lead it into the future.

EARLY SETTLERS

Character, hard work, and ideas drove several major community innovations throughout the years. The earliest settlers did not have crock pots, cars, or electricity. They arrived from all over the South: from Tennessee to Texas and from the Blue Ridge Mountains, and Alabama. They worked hard and built log cabins—like the Abe Lincolns further north in Illinois, Indiana, and Kentucky. The communities rallied together, as they do today.

GONE TO TEXAS

DALLAS GOT IT RIGHT!

TEXAS LONGHORN

A Texas cattleman in the 1800s, Sam Maverick was known for refusing to brand his cattle, more interested in keeping track of the land he owned than the livestock on it.

The Texas Longhorn made more history than any other breed of cattle the world has known. These wiry, intractable beasts were themselves pioneers in a harsh land, moving elementally with drought, grass, Arctic blizzards, and burning winds. Their story is the bedrock on which the history of the cow country rests.

KING COTTON

Dallas is a city built on cotton, cows, oil, military, retail, wholesaling, industrial marketing, and computer technology. Today, its towns and cities are overflowing with entrepreneurs in a variety of industries from film, to development, to consumer goods. The corridor by Dallas Fort Worth airport is a hub of commercial warehouse activity that includes retail giant amazon.com. All global roads lead to Dallas, and it holds the distinction of being the second largest area for Fortune 500 companies headquarters, after New York. We predict that will change very soon and Dallas will move to #1.

Steamboats carried cotton from Jefferson in east Texas on the Red River down to New Orleans and on to Liverpool, England.

Cotton fiber launched the Industrial Revolution with factories around Manchester and Birmingham, England. An agricultural age became an industrial age

Dallas Cotton Exchange bought cotton from farmers, and was key to pricing, shipping, marketing and banking. Merchants bought cotton from farmers. Cotton remained "king" of North Texas agricultural products until World War II. By 1940, brokers at the Dallas Cotton Exchange were handling 2.5 million bales each year. America's biggest export crop was cotton.

Today's Mansion on Turtle Creek was the "mansion" of a cotton merchant named Sheppard King. It was later owned by the local Wyly family, and finally transformed to its current splendor by Caroline Rose Hunt.

A New England Yankee migrant to North Carolina named Eli Whitney invented the cotton gin working on the plantation of a South Carolina Revolutionary General. The gin, plus the steamboat (which could power people up river—not just drift downriver on a raft), were the two key technologies that made the Southern states into a cotton kingdom from 1800 to 1860.

Later, as cotton moved west, Dallas became the biggest maker of cotton gins.

NATCHITOCHES

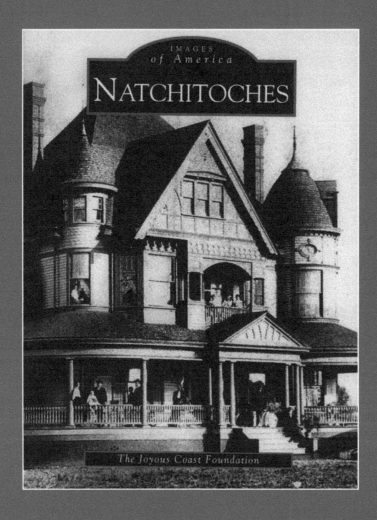

The oldest permanent settlement in the Louisiana Purchase founded in 1714 by French Canadian, Louis Juchereau de St. Denis, who was enroute to Mexico from Mobile, Alabama and stopped in the area occupied by the Natchitoches Indians.

The movie *Steel Magnolias* was filmed in Natchitoches.

Thomas Jefferson paid 3¢ an acre for the middle one-third of today's U.S.A. The seller was Napoleon's France, who needed the money to invade and conquer the English. The Dutch extended a loan and the rest is history!

A Texas Longhorn stands by Alfred Membreno, who went to Highland Park High School with Sam's daughter, Kelly O'Donovan.

Preston Trail, which crossed Trinity River at the spot that became Dallas, was first an Indian trail, then a trail to drive cows north to market in Missouri or Kansas. Today it's called Preston Road, an active route for residents, executives and families commuting to the office, schools, or a variety of events. When the earliest settlers arrived, could they have imagined what has been built today? Preston is a trail that has seen a thousand lifetimes. Families, generation upon generation, lives and ideas and businesses and people traveling along.

The cattle trails ran up from South Texas and split into the Shawnee that ran through Fort Worth and the Preston that ran through Dallas. The longhorns crossed Dallas Trinity River and up Preston Road to Fort Preston on Oklahoma 's Red River. Some went on to Sedalia Missouri railhead.

The Red River, a 1948 movie, starred Jo Anne Dru, John Wayne, and Montgomery Clift.

TRANSPORTATION

Algorithm map of commute to work time and distance. DFW metro is tight versus its major competitors.

Carriages

Horses and wagons brought many to Dallas. The rugged spirit of the earliest settlers, and the heart of the cowboy lives on in these territories, today. The wagons have been replaced by lamborghinis, Mercedes and minivans, as well as electric cars. What will the future hold?

The family carriage was a common sight in early Texas towns.

Street Cars

Street cars traveled past our Beverly house (then the Schoellkopfs) and went out to Southern Methodist University (SMU.) This downtown street car image was taken in September 1948 when President Harry Truman visited Dallas. A guy from Independence, Missouri, Truman followed Franklin Roosevelt of New York. Next would be Eisenhower, born in Denison, Texas.

Railroads

The arrival of the railroads to Dallas in 1872 was the key event in the development of the city, turning it almost overnight into a boomtown.

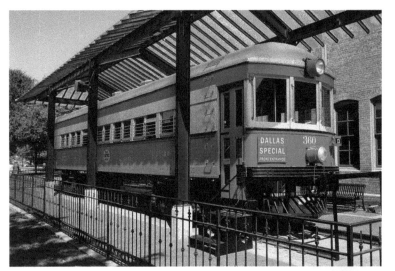

Interurban Train

Interurban rail lines carried passengers on electrically powered trains to communities such as Sherman, Denison, McKinney, Fort Worth, Corsicana, and Waco.

Model T

A tribute to the 1908 Model T, the machine that put America on wheels.

COLORADO

Centennial, Colorado, founded on the USA's 100th birthday in 1876 is the focus of James Michener's great bestselling novel *Centennial* and is about driving cattle North, Arapaho Indians, German immigrants from Lancaster, Pennsylvania, and an Englishman 's investment in 5,000,000 ranch acres and Jim Lloyd, a Texas cowboy, and "Potato" Brumbaugh, a German immigrant from Russia protecting his water rights.

We bought our Woody Creek Ranch near Aspen's Roaring Fork River from a descendant of Italian immigrants who came for the silver mining boom and stayed to farm when the silver was gone. We named it "Rosemary's Ranch." She and her children built houses there.

Kim and Evan's wedding was at Rosemary's house on Woody Creek Ranch.

THE ALAMO

Uncle Christopher A. Parker was one of the 187 heroes of the Alamo. He rode his horse from Natchez, Mississippi to help Texas fight for independence. Christiana is named for him. He had been educated "back East," sold his land to his sister, Minerva, and her husband Edward Sparrow, left his handwritten will in 1835, and signed the Goliad Texas Declaration of Independence.

Uncle Alfred Wyly was captain of a 20-man company in Sam Houston's Texas Army of fellow Tennesseans who helped Texas fight for independence. Alfred's company and their horses towed the "Twin Sisters" cannon—a gift to the Texans from Cincinnati, "The Queen City of the West."

700 Texans at San Jacinto, the earlier Battle of New Orleans, and the Oregon Trail, led to the USA growing from coast to coast.

Hollywood actor John Wayne spent years trying to get Hollywood to film the great epic, finally getting it done by working for free. Wayne was lead actor and producer of the 1960 film *The Alamo*. John Wayne collaborated with one of his closest friends, James Edward Grant, a writer who owned a cattle ranch.

It's fair to say that Texas and the American West are the grandchildren of Andrew Jackson's lieutenants—Sam Houston (who was wounded at the Battle of Horseshoe Bend) and James K. Polk (who ran for president on the issue of whether Texas should be part of the United States).

Our story is about values and growth, starting with John Neely Bryan, also from Tennessee, and his log cabin. Neely sold a few lots for people to build their log cabin or farm.

JEFFERSON

The town of Jefferson in East Texas floated cotton down the Red River to the Mississippi to New Orleans before there was a Dallas. Jay Gould wanted to build a railroad through Jefferson, but the citizens said, "No, we don't want a smelly railroad."

Gould prophesied "Grass will grow in the streets of Jefferson." The people of Jefferson were saying "no" to economic development.

The T&P Railway (Texas and Pacific) built a transcontinental railroad from Marshall, Texas, westward. There was no Dallas or Fort Worth before it.

The Sam Wyly family took a lot of family trips on the rivers of middle America. On the trip to Nashville, you have to go through locks that raise the water level at dams on the Tennessee. Without such, there would be no lakes in Texas (except Caddo Lake) and less city water and electricity.

KRUM

Teacher, Hattie Dyer, who taught for nearly 40 years, instructed generations of Krum families.

The rich prairie soil produced bountiful wheat harvest that became famous. In the early 1900s, Krum was the largest wagon grain market in the Unites States. Over a million pounds of grain were shipped out in 1900. The Chicago Board of Trade called every morning to ask about prices and volumes.

The wheat won a grand prize in the 1904 St. Louis World's fair.

Krum's prosperity supported a hotel, 24 commercial businesses, two gins, two grain elevators, and one up-to-date flour mill. Its low, rolling hills provided beauty as well as fertility. Krum felt justified in advertising itself (on city letterhead) as the "Garden Spot of Denton County."

The Methodist Church was organized in 1876 with 10 charter members in the one-room schoolhouse. Upon outgrowing the one-room schoolhouse, a new church was built at a cost of $2,000.

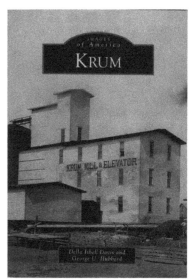

MARSHALL

Wiley College's Debate Team became National Champs by defeating USC's debate team in the 1930s. It was depicted in the movie, *The Great Debaters* with Denzel Washington.

James Farmer, one of the Wiley debaters, was a member of the Presidential Advisory Commission for Nixon and Ford and on which Sam served as chairman. This commission had the CEO of General Motors and several other great men representing Americas largest companies.

Sam and President Nixon with Advisory Commission leaders at the White House. Fourth from the left is Alan Steelman, who beat Dallas mayor Earle Cabell to become the first Republican from Dallas's 5th district.

EAST TEXAS

Wiley debate team ready for historic rematch

Schools featured in movie have changed since '35 competition

By JAMES RAGLAND
Staff Writer
jragland@dallasnews.com

Cary Chavis knows the stakes will be high when he takes the stage Friday night for a historic debate at Wiley College in Marshall.

He tries to block out the hype, he said, so the symbolic weight of the moment doesn't overwhelm him.

"But it really kind of puts everything into perspective — the school's legacy, the country's history, the significance of what happened in 1935," said the senior debate captain.

That's the year Wiley, a small historically black college, knocked off the University of Southern California's top-ranked debate team.

On Friday, nearly 77 years after Wiley's stunning victory, the two schools will face each other again in Marshall.

But this time, rather than a black duo facing a white one, both squads will project just how different America is today.

The Wiley team features a white male from Houston and Chavis, who is black, from Lake Charles, La. USC's exhibition

'Wiley College
From left: The 1935 debate team at Wiley College consisted of Hobart Jarrett, Henry Heights and James Farmer Jr.

MELVIN B. TOLSON assembled Wiley's 1930s teams.

team boasts two females, one white and the other with roots in India.

"Back in 1935, it was interesting because we left the building as equals. And this time, we're entering the building as equals," said Christopher Medina, the school's director of forensics.

It's a poignant moment in history for Wiley, which revived its moribund debate team in 2008, the year after the school was featured in the 2007 Denzel Washington movie *The Great Debaters.*

Washington and other donors gave the school roughly $1.5 million to resuscitate the forensics program.

When the schools first met, the country was deeply "divided by a color line," noted Dr. Haywood L. Strickland, president and chief executive officer of Wiley.

"I am proud that years later, these sch meet in a country t brates differences, kn skin color is no detern intelligence and re that we share a comm manity," Strickland sai

That was not the c Melvin B. Tolson — black English professor assembled Wiley's pow

debate teams in the 1930s.

His squads gained a hard-earned reputation for being unbeatable, and many schools were afraid to face them.

Given the country's racial segregation at the time, the Wiley team members typically packed themselves into an older-model car, traveling along back roads and streets to reach their destinations. They avoided white-owned hotels and restaurants that forbade them.

Fast-forward to 2012 and one now finds a Wiley College that's emphasizing diversity, as evidenced by the mixed team that will take the stage on Friday and the Hispanic debate coach recently hired to direct it.

"I had other offers to go to other schools," said Chad Mossman, a senior from Houston and the only white debater at Wiley. "But I wanted to go somewhere that was different, unique."

Mossman, a business student, hopes to go to law school when he graduates from Wiley, a place, he said, where he's been warmly embraced by his peers and professors.

He said attending Wiley and joining the debate team has been a great experience. "I have never regretted it," Mossman said.

That is a familiar refrain heard around the Wiley cam

beginning to rebound when Hollywood came calling.

Washington's $1 million gift to the school, combined with roughly half a million dollars in pledges from other donors, helped get the debate program off the ground and fueled the school's revival.

Chavis saw *The Great Debaters* with his family on Christmas Day in 2007. He was so moved by the film that he decided Wiley was where he needed to be.

"I didn't know about the Denzel Washington money until I got here," said Chavis, whose debating skills helped earn him a full scholarship.

The Wiley team ranked in the top 10 in the 2011 Pi Kappa Delta National Tournament and third in debate sweepstakes, said Medina.

For Chavis, who has participated in "80 to 100 debates"

Sam introducing Joe Kirven to President Nixon. Sam loved the movie—it brought back his own memories on the debate team at LA Tech—and long rides on a yellow school bus to colleges in the "ARK-LA-TEX."

Sam managed the Nixon presidential campaign in Texas.

OKLAHOMA AND TEXAS TOWNS

Boom Town is a movie that depicts Oklahoma and Texas towns such as Burkburnett, Electra, Kilgore, Corsicana and Borger. Electra, the "Pump Jack Capital of America" was named for granddaughter of W. T. Waggoner, who found oil on his huge ranch near Vernon in 1903—over a half million acres.

Route 66 was officially decertified in 1985 as the newer interstate system that paralleled a lot of earlier highways (like Sam's Highway 80), was put in place across the U.S.A.

The Magnolia gas station was one of the first encountered by westbound travelers entering Texas on Route 66 from Chicago. Magnolia became Mobile, which became Exxon-Mobile, and moved its headquarters from New York City to Dallas in 1989.

ROUTE 66 IN TEXAS, OKLAHOMA AND MISSOURI

BRIDGES

This legendary bridge connects Natchez, Mississippi to Ferriday, Louisiana and is a parade route for the annual Memorial Day parade. As of the writing of this book, the bridge is closed for two years for repair. At flood times, rivers and bayous half-cover houses and reach up to the bridges.

DALLAS GOT IT RIGHT!

Margaret Hunt Hill Bridge

AN AMERICAN STORY

Young Katy Cleland sails from Scotland in 1657 and lands on the shores of Chesapeake Bay in the Maryland Colony. John Balch, originally from Somerset County, England, arrives soon thereafter.

Katy marries John, a fellow Presbyterian, in 1659. They settle on Deer Creek.

Katy and John's 20-year-old son, Tom, briefly returns to England in 1685, where he is recruited by the Duke of Monmouth to fight in his unsuccessful rebellion against King James II. Grandson Hezekiah Balch graduates Princeton in 1762, preaches and teaches in log colleges in Pennsylvania, Virginia, and North Carolina, and founds the first college in Tennessee.

ANCESTORS

Sam's great-great-granddad, Edward Sparrow, was born in Dublin, Ireland. He was educated by his older brother, William, founder of Kenyon College in Ohio. He moved to Natchez in 1835.

He married Minerva Parker, sister of our "Hero of the Alamo." Uncle Christopher refused to surrender by taking with them 600 troops of the invading Mexican dictator, already weakened by rebels in Zacateus and Goliad.

Lake Providence, where Sam was born, had Germans, Italians, Jews, Chinese, Africans, and French Huguenots. True to our Mark Twain-described history as a steamboat stop on the Mississippi River, everyone was from somewhere else.

King George III said, "Don't call it an American Revolution. Call it a Presbyterian Revolution."

Uncle Alfred Wyly

Hezekiah Balch

Baby Rosemary Catherine is the newest member of the Wyly clan.

Katy, granddaddy Charles Samuel Wyly, Ethel, Charles Joseph Wyly, and Mumzell

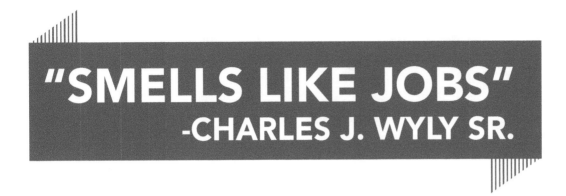

"SMELLS LIKE JOBS"
-CHARLES J. WYLY SR.

Early on, Texas and Louisiana forests were a big resource for lumber and for paper.

Jonesboro and Bastrop, Louisiana had paper mills. When we'd drive through towns that had a paper mill, there was a very strong smell. Mama would say, "This town stinks."

Dad would say, "Smells like jobs."

A lot of these towns were the ones that built the high schools in many of the surrounding areas. It was the saw mills that produced the cut logs that created the lumber to build schools and houses.

HORSE JUMPING

On the Charles Wyly side of the family, it was Emily's interest to jump horses. They eventually sold the ranch to the Tillersons.

Rex Tillerson's wife Renda St. Clair also jumps horses at their ranch in Bartonville, a beautiful country town north of DFW.

EAST TEXAS

My road to Dallas was Highway 80.

Lady Bird Johnson came to Dallas' St. Ann School for Girls. Her parents came to North Texas from Alabama. Lady Bird's retired secretary gets her morning latte in Highland Park Village.

Don Henley of the Eagles is from Karnack in East Texas. One of the first things he did when he made some money was to contribute to the protection of Caddo Lake, the only natural lake in the State of Texas. All others were man-made.

The Eagles were early back-up singers for Linda Ronstadt.

Linda lived next door to our Malibu Colony beach house.

Caddo Lake

THE DELHI DISPATCH

Sam Wyly drove with his dad to Jonesville in East Texas to buy a second-hand printing press so *The Delhi Dispatch* could stop outsourcing the paper printing.

The Wylys were also the telegraph agency, where petroleum engineers in the oil fields messaged what's coming to be refined.

FARMING

Texans like their trucks, and the Wylys were loyal to Ford trucks and John Deere tractors. The back end of the bed of a Ford pickup has been used to haul hay bales from the old feed store in small towns like Keller, Texas, that have exploded in population over the years. Residents still drive pickups, and several in towns all across the Dallas area and beyond still haul hay for their horses. Feed stores, farming equipment, and a strong country feel still permeate the state.

THE BIRTH OF THE INTERNET

Sam's Datran tower.
Twenty-two miles line of sight to beam digital radio signals to Frisco from Cedar Hill.
The beginning of a digital backbone for what would ultimately be called "the internet."

MAGNOLIA PETROLEUM

Bill Clements' company was South Eastern Drilling Company. He drilled oil wells in the southeast, the southwest, and offshore. After his career, he turned to public service and was the first Republican governor of Texas since the Civil War.

From Gov. Clements' office, Jim Francis helped build the modern Republican party in Texas. What had once been the Democratic solid south was becoming the Republican solid south.

Rex Tillerson, born in Wichita Falls, TX, also made the move from his career at Exxon-Mobil to public service when he became Secretary of State in 2017.

BONHAM TO PLANO STAGECOACH

Dallas includes dozens of out-lying cities such as Addison, Arlington, Bonham, El Paso, Fort Worth, Waco, North-South from College Station to Oklahoma; Weatherford, West White Sands proving ground; Downtown, Uptown, Frisco, Plano, Grand Prairie, Fort Bliss, Texarkana, Oak Cliff, Preston Hollow, Southlake, and Farmers Branch. There is a diverse population across this area, of varying nationalities, races and incomes.

One of the wealthiest small towns in the state, Westlake, is a sister city to Southlake, with a waiting list to get into the school. Residents who want their kids to attend the prestigious Westlake Academy must enter a lottery, and often wait years. Westlake is surrounded by property near the Ross Perot ranch, and the Fidelity headquarters.

EAST TEXAS

Sam grew up on the bayou, the very low part. Gas was 11 cents per gallon! Today it's significantly higher in every town in America.

Dr. Pepper was invented at a Waco drugstore in 1885 by Charles Alderton, a young pharmacist. It was purchased by a Dallas company in 1898. The drink is now a global sensation and is sold in countries across the world including South Africa and New Zealand.

COMANCHE INDIAN NATION

Comanche Nation in Wyoming migrated south through Colorado, Kansas, Oklahoma, and New Mexico to West Texas in the 1740s.

They became the most fierce horse warriors—able to fire an arrow or bullet from under their horses' bellies at full gallop.

In their 50-year war with the Texas Rangers, the Comanche made their last stand in Palo Dura Canyon, reminding us Scots of George Washington saying, "If I am defeated on all other fronts, I will make my last stand among the Scotch-Irish of the Shenandoah Valley of Virginia."

EDUCATION

Dallas is a major center of education that continues to build leaders who go on to graduate and make global contributions. The Dallas Independent School District is one of the largest in the country, far from its humble beginnings in one-room schoolhouses. Today these schools include Thomas Jefferson High, to the Booker T. Washington School for the Performing and Visual Arts located in the Arts District of downtown Dallas, known for educating several famous accomplished performers and artists. And there are magnet schools for science that teach special skills such as nursing.

JUAREZ SCHOOL IN DALLAS

Was in Little Mexico—now covered by free-ways, skyscrapers and high rise apartments.

IMAGES
of America

DALLAS'S
LITTLE MEXICO

Sol Villasana

Benito Juarez was the "George Washington of Mexico."

SCHOOLS

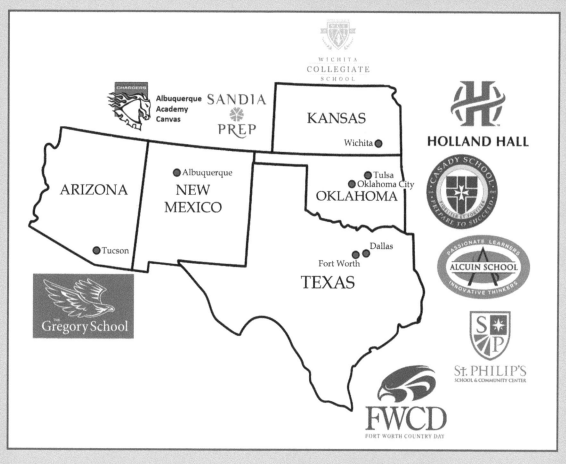

DELHI HIGH SCHOOL

Sam's Dad's headline in *The Delhi Dispatch*, December 19, 1951:

"DHS Bears Win State Grid Title"

In the 1940s, Delhi was the center of a large natural gas boom.

Oil field jobs brought in new families from Arkansas, Oklahoma, and Texas. Monroe Fowler, the big, Cherokee who was a lineman beside said, "We were oil field trash, but when Sam took me to his parent's house—I could feel the educated gentility of the Old South. I would never have got to college without the football scholarship that really came from stories written by Sam's dad published in all the state's big newspapers and heard on the radio. That attracted college coaches." Monroe had a great career in the Army.

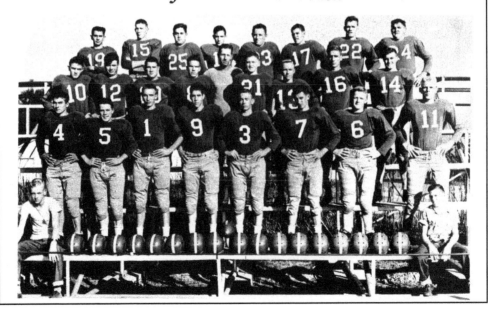

Delhi 1951 High
Class B State Champions
Raymond Richards - Coach

AT TECH, MY DREAM JOB WAS TO BE A FORESTER

Pictured above with Sam are Mama, Rosemary and Louisiana Tech president, Jay Taylor.

Sam would be in a tower in the forest watching out for fires, have time to read a lot of books, and with good luck from Mother Nature on rains and winds, rarely have to actively fight a forest fire.

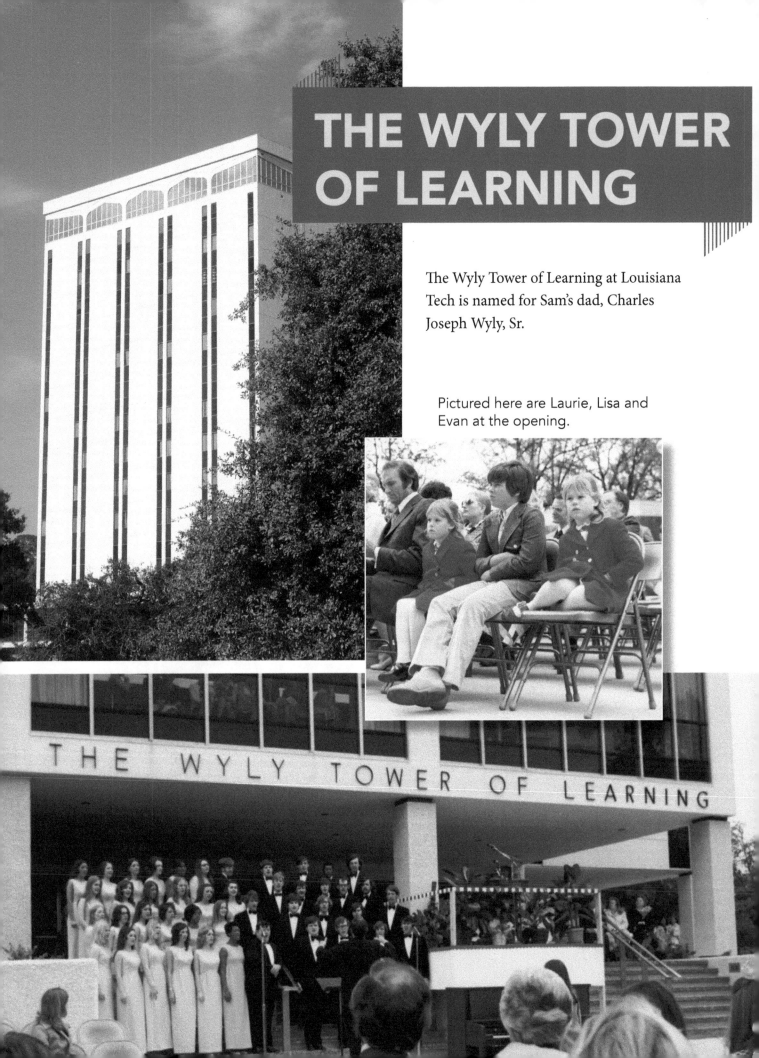

THE WYLY TOWER OF LEARNING

The Wyly Tower of Learning at Louisiana Tech is named for Sam's dad, Charles Joseph Wyly, Sr.

Pictured here are Laurie, Lisa and Evan at the opening.

COLLEGES

HIGHLAND PARK ATHLETES & SOLDIERS AND SAILORS

HIGHLAND PARK HIGH SCHOOL
Enter to learn. Go forth to serve.

Highland Park is the best public high school in the State of Texas. Established in 1915, this school has a long history of success and celebrated graduates.

Four years after walking across the stage together at Highland Park High School, Myer Ungerman, Blake Gordon, and Hardy Davis took military oaths. Ungerman and Gordon graduated from the US Military Academy, and Davis graduated from the US Naval Academy.

Edgemere's Janet and George Clayton's granddaughters cheer for Highland Park.

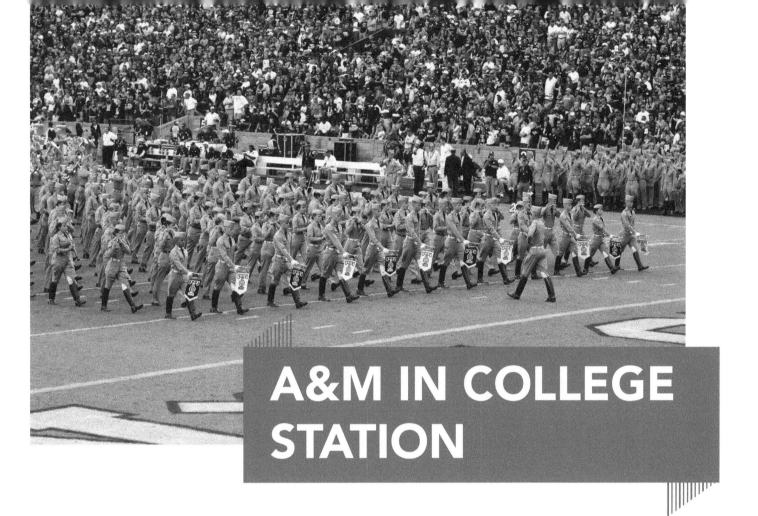

A&M IN COLLEGE STATION

General Patton said, "Give me an army of West Point grads and I'll win a battle. Give me an army of Texas Aggies and I'll win a war."

Texas A&M was a land grant school, just like Louisiana Tech, created to train the farmers and the mechanics. Every state already had at least one literary and arts school. The Morrill Act gave federal lands to establish colleges that trained students for practical work, and every freshman boy was in the military service for a minimum of two years.

GRANDDADDY WYLY

Son of an 1836 Princeton grad; Presbyterian minister; law clerk for Louisiana Supreme Court, he managed plantation land along the lakes, bayous and rivers. He took steamboat to Baton Rouge from Lake Providence for lawmaking. Valedictorian of University of Tennessee in Knoxville in 1876.

Yours Truly,

THE ARTS

Vibrant cultural and arts districts abound. El Paso, Lubbock, Abilene, Fort Worth, Plano, Oklahoma City, Tulsa, Little Rock, and Kansas City all have wonderfully developed areas that celebrate the arts, culture, history, and science.

In downtown Dallas alone, one will find the Nasher Sculpture Center, Crow Collection of Asian Art, Dallas Museum of Art, Winspear Opera House, Morton Meyerson Symphony Center, Dallas Black Dance Theater, Dallas Theater Center, Perot Museum of Nature and Science, Wyly Theatre and more.

Sam's mama, Flora (who had been a one-time New York City dancer) was the inspiration for all the Wylys' artistic endeavors.

When visitors come to see Sam, he often steers them to Fort Worth to see all the different museums. They have the Kimball, Amon Carter, Modern Art, National Cowgirl, and Sid Richardson, to name a few.

MUSICIANS

Texarkana's Scott Joplin, "King of Ragtime Music," – early 1900s – from Texarkana.

As a cultural hotbed, Dallas and the surrounding areas has been the home to many live music venues, concerts, and musicians. Several big name musicians have graced the stage of the American Airlines Center, and many local musical greats have gotten their start performing at the House of Blues. From the Symphony to the Orchestra to the music programs inside high schools, Dallas got it right!

MUSIC

Eryka Badu

Kelly Clarkson

Selena Gomez

Steve Miller

Stevie Ray Vaughan

Tim Delaughter -
Polyphonic Spree

Willie Nelson

From the House of Blues to live music in the park, Dallas is a hotbed of musical genius. Nearly every suburb large or small has a schedule of summer music concerts featuring new talent, from the city square in Denton, near The University of North Texas, to the newest development at Lakeside, near the Dallas Fort Worth airport. Many musical careers have been cultivated in Dallas.

The Wyly Theatre

Over 500 plays are performed at the Kalita Humphreys Theater, including Samson and Delilah—a romance of Biblical proportions. The audience can sit up close to the actors. It's a beautiful way to experience the theater.

It and other local playhouses were the predecessors of the Wyly Theatre on Flora Street in downtown Dallas.

Bible stories became sculpture as well as paintings. Our *Samson & Delilah* statue was carved from stone in Rome in 1850s by a native born American.

DALLAS THEATER

WEATHERFORD, TEXAS

Mary Martin and Larry Hagman

Hagman's mom, Mary Martin, was America's top Broadway star. When Sam Wyly was a teenager, his mother took him and his brother Charles Jr. to see Mary Martin on Broadway.

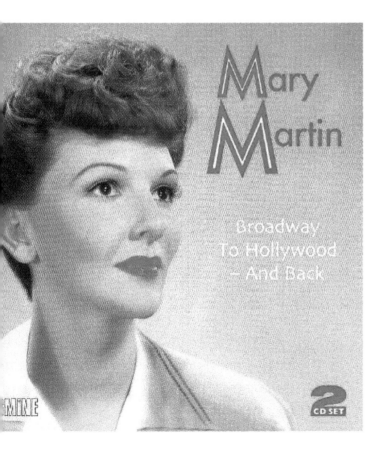

Larry Hagman as "JR" in "Dallas," an American prime time television soap opera that ran all over the world for 13 years filmed at Southfork Ranch.

BIG SPRING

Stephan Pyles was born in Big Spring, West Texas.

Pyles is a founding father of Southwestern cuisine, blending elements of Southern home-style cooking, sophisticated Southwestern fare, Mexican food, and Tex-Mex food, as well as Cajun cuisine and Creole cookery.

A fifth-generation Texan, his many talents and endeavors have garnered him numerous awards. Pyles is a chef, cookbook author, philanthropist, and educator.

His Restaurant at "The Wyly Theatre" in downtown Dallas

INNOVATION AND BUSINESS

For more than 175 years, Dallas has been at the center of business and innovation. The Dallas-Fort Worth metroplex (roughly the size of New Hampshire) is home to some of the largest companies in America.

ONLY IN AMERICA

Only in America could the shale revolution in oil and gas production have happened. The USA's unique laws that go back to our state and national homestead acts grant landowners not only the use of their property, but everything below. In the rest of the world, you find government ownership and control of these mineral rights. Here, any company can lease these rights and start drilling. This Darwinian competition between entrepreneurs has created our 12,000 independent producers and associated service providers. Texas A&M, LSU, and OU train petroleum engineers and geologists, and geophysicists.

China and Europe may sit on vast reserves, but they will never catch us. In the ten years since the fracking boom began, we have invested $1 trillion and drilled 150,000 horizontal wells versus only a few 100 in the rest of the world. Unlike Texans, Okies and Cajuns, like me, who have grown up in the oil fields, people in most other countries lack knowledge of the benefits or the hard work and smart work needed to succeed, because the state-owned oil companies drill mostly in deep offshore waters or in remote onshore lands. It's easy to have a "not in my backyard" attitude if the only beneficiaries are government bureaucrats.

The United States has not only individual ownership of the land and the companies (thank you, Thomas Jefferson), but also open capital markets and a reasonable regulatory system (thank you, John Marshall) that have generated innovation and technology that other countries can only dream of. The result: not only three million more well paid jobs in the next ten years, but also a $750 a year cost of living reduction for every family that drives a car and lower electricity costs, for everybody, plus cleaner air from cleaner energy as we shut down dirty old coal plants all over the United States while China and India build more to add to the choking air pollution in their cities.

KARL MARX GOT IT WRONG; ADAM SMITH GOT IT RIGHT.

ALLEN

Money magazine listed this town in Texas as one of the Best Places to Live in 2017. This town along with several other Texas cities such as Flower Mound and University Park, have consistently been named as the best small towns to raise a family in.

Growth is the buzzword around Allen, an affluent suburb north almost to Oklahoma. The city of 96,000 residents has worked to actively create economic opportunities within its borders, and the efforts are bearing fruit: Allen has seen $1.6 billion of development breaking ground in 2017 alone. A number of tech and cybersecurity companies have recently committed to the area, bringing with them hundreds of jobs.

Data company, Cyrus One, recently purchased 66 acres of land to support an expected $1 billion data campus in Allen in the coming years.

A $91 million convention center and hotel complex will start serving patrons in 2018, while international real estate firm, Hines, recently announced plans for the Strand, a 135-acre mixed-use development that will bring office space, retail outlets, residential options, and a greenbelt and waterway.

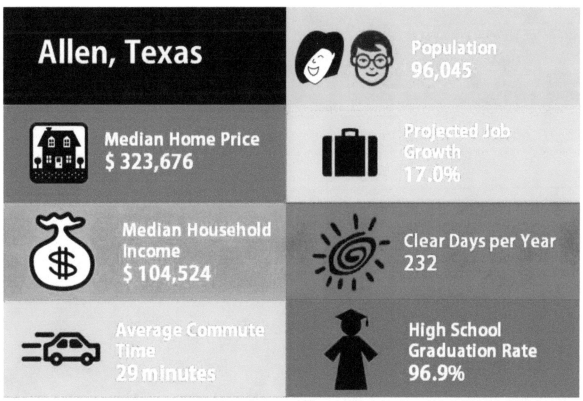

Allen, Texas

Population 96,045

Median Home Price $ 323,676

Projected Job Growth 17.0%

Median Household Income $ 104,524

Clear Days per Year 232

Average Commute Time 29 minutes

High School Graduation Rate 96.9%

SOURCES: Synergos Technologies, realtor.com, Moody's Analytics, National Oceanic and Atmospheric Administration, and Department of Education.

MULESHOE

Mule powered windmill in Muleshoe, Texas.

The locals in Muleshoe may have been ahead of their time. **Green Mountain Energy** convinced Texas to go for "Clean Air Through Clean Energy."

Texas now produces more natural gas, more wind, and more solar energy than the next several states combined.

The cost of electricity in Dallas is half of the cost in New York City.

Green Mountain Energy®

The early oil days included exploring up near Oklahoma in North Texas. Clint Murchison Sr. and Sid Richardson grew up together in Athens, Texas. They first got into the oil business in west Texas. Sid had no heirs and left a large donation to his foundation and to his nephew, Perry Richardson Bass of Fort Worth. They were Wildcatters, roughnecks and pipeline guys. Sam grew up in the Delhi Oil Field and had a summer job working on building pipelines. He rode to work in the back end of a truck, and he loves today's TV ads for trucks on televised football games.

Sam's first education on Texas Wildcatters and "hostile takeovers" on Wall Street was a *Time* magazine article on July 26, 1954 titled, "Railroads: Wheel of a Deal." Sam's newspaper editor dad got a big laugh of two oil patch guys taking control of a railroad from the Wall Streeters in New York City. This was a prelude to Boone Pickens' drilling for oil on Wall Street funded by Mike Milken's "junk bonds." Wylys were backers of Boone and Mike.

Magnolia Petroleum building was the tallest building west of the
Mississippi at 29 floors. It's double-sided, neon-red Pegasus, "the flying
red horse," towered over the skyline.

Before the largest oil discovery in Texas in the early 1900s, everything was controlled out of the northeast. Magnolia was the first Texas oil company to compete with the east. Jim Francis' granddad, as general counsel for Magnolia, was a part of the organizing that developed into Magnolia.

HUMBLE OIL BECAME EXXON

Sam's job offers included companies recruiting from Louisiana Tech, just like colleges recruit for students in Dallas high schools today. This is an offer letter from Humble Oil. Sam also had an offer from IBM. After graduate school and after military training, he went to work for IBM.

HUMBLE OIL & REFINING COMPANY
EMPLOYEE RELATIONS DEPARTMENT
HOUSTON 1, TEXAS

K. R. DAILEY
MANAGER
J. N. BEASLEY, JR.
WILLIAM GRANT, JR.
ASSISTANT MANAGERS
R. B. ROAPER
SAFETY
T. W. MOORE
TRAINING
R. N. DYER
PERSONNEL
W. H. HAINES
ANNUITIES AND BENEFITS
PAUL V. LUCAS
SALARY AND WAGE

June 8, 1956

Mr. Samuel Evans Wyly
Box 725
Delhi, Louisiana

Dear Mr. Wyly:

This will confirm the offer of employment made to you by the Controller's Department management at a starting salary of $385. For your information, present policy permits an increase of $35 per month at the end of one year of satisfactory service. This increase is not a part of the regular merit increase program.

Employment with this Company is contingent upon good health; therefore, we desire that you undergo a medical examination by a physician of your choice at our expense. We are enclosing a medical examination form for this purpose as well as an introductory letter to the physician. The examining physician should mail the completed form, together with his bill, as soon as possible to our Medical Division. Your medical fitness will be determined from this report.

Should you accept this offer, the Humble Company will defray all reasonable expenses in excess of $50 in connection with moving your household effects, your personal and family transportation, and lodging and meals from your present location to Houston.

It will be appreciated if you will advise as soon as possible whether or not you accept this offer, indicating the date that you can conveniently report.

We hope that you will accept this offer, and we look forward to hearing from you.

Yours very truly,

R. N. DYER, Head
Personnel Division

RND:mmm
Enclosures

Sam's offer letter from Humble Oil & Refining Company in 1956

H.L. HUNT FAMILIES

"For years I had thought about going south to an area of the Mississippi River Delta about which my father had told me many stories," said H. L. Hunt. "My father told me of the unbelievably rich, alluvial soil in this delta country. So, I started south in 1912, going to the little town of Lake Village, Arkansas."

Hunt bought a 960-acre plantation on Bayou Boeuf which means "Beef River" in French. France owned the middle third of America until 1803—then sold to Thomas Jefferson's regime for 3 cents an acre—the Louisiana Purchase.

Some were in awe of H. L. Hunt's insistence that his children do "real work" and that they learn the business from the ground up. "He did have that opinion, but he really didn't force it on any of us," Ray Hunt said. "June, Helen and Swanee (his sisters) all worked on the switchboard and did other jobs around the Dallas office. Dad did not have to cajole or twist arms. I think all of us felt that it was a real privilege and an opportunity."

Swanee Hunt is a teacher of Public Policy at Harvard and a former United States Ambassador to Austria.

Granddaddy H. L. Hunt as a young man in a straw hat, *The History of Hunt Oil Company, Our 60th Year, 1994*

SUSTAINABLE FARMIING

Texas A&M's Norman Borlaug led worldwide initiatives that contributed to the extensive increases in agricultural production. His work created foods that helped millions across the world learn how to create and grow sustainable foods.

Christiana Wyly married Kimbal Musk, who has been credited with spearheading and promoting the farm to table movement to "grow and eat more plants." Kimbal co-founded The Kitchen Community, a nonprofit with locations in Colorado and Memphis. Christiana is passionate about the environment and healthy foods and has been since childhood. In the picture above she's wearing her dad's Future Farmers of America jacket from high school days.

MICHAELS STORES

Michaels is the largest arts and craft retailer in the nation with 1,360 stores giving artists and families a place to learn, create and grow through various supplies, craft classes and projects. Wyly grew a handful of Dallas-area stores in 1983 to more than 770 nationwide stores by 2002. The typical customer was a woman with kids who bought five items for $20 for an Indian Princess or Boy Scout event. Sam sold Michaels in a $6 billion private equity deal with Bain and Blackstone in 2006.

Michaels China Story:

My son-in-law David Matthews and I visited a plant on the Chinese mainland where 1500 young women were hand-painting silk flowers that we imported and sold in our Michaels chain for $5. We couldn't have made that flower in America for $50. Actually, we couldn't have made it at all. What they were doing on the Chinese mainland, they had once done in Hong Kong. The work moved to mainland China because people in Hong Kong could earn more money in the higher value-added tasks that were developing there. Earlier, this same kind of work had moved out of Japan to Hong Kong. If you traced it all the way back, you could see how this work got pushed out of Tennessee and made its way to Japan.

This story is told currently in a movie, *Outsourced*, with a lot of belly laughs and a love story.

Doug Sullivan got great locations all over the United States and always had several local developers competing to get a Michaels as an anchor store in their shopping strip. Michaels never went to malls.

Today, Sullivan is a pastor at Park Cities Baptist Church. His brilliant wife and daughters used to come hiking by our Beverly house.

Store managers in front of the single Dallas warehouse, today eight "distribution centers" USA-wide serve 1365 stores.

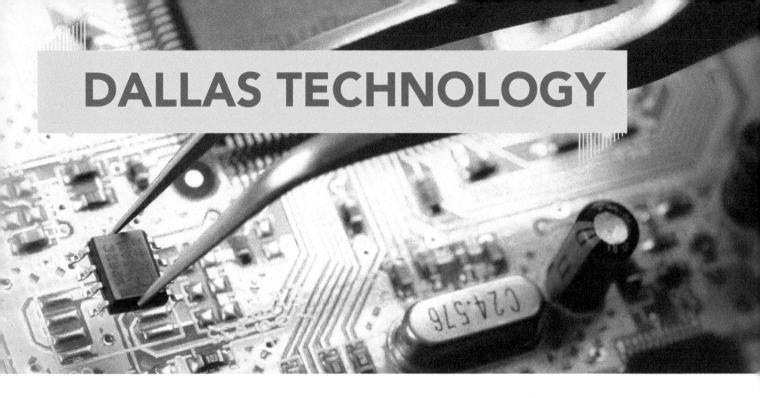

DALLAS TECHNOLOGY

Texas Instruments (TI) is a multi-national technology company founded and headquartered in Dallas. Jack Kilby, a TI engineer, got a Nobel Prize for inventing the computer chip.

"Chips" produced by TI are in cell phones around the world.

Texas Instruments was started as a geophysical services company to do "doodle bugging" for oil producers. Dynamite was exploded underground from three or more locations and the reflected sound waves read to "map" the different layers of different kinds of rock in the Earth's surface. Their technology has and continues to add to America's ability to reduce violence and increase productivity around the world.

Today, Texas Instruments is a global technology company that designs and sells internal computer tech to designers and manufacturers all over the world.

Sam Wyly roughnecked in the Delhi Oil Fields as a summer job and this motivated him to take geology as a science class at Louisiana Tech which helped him start up University Computing to serve petroleum engineers..

The University of Texas at Dallas was created by the founders of Texas Instruments, Eugene McDermott, Cecil Green, Eric Jonsson, and Pat Haggerty.

UCC

Erik Jonsson was Brooklyn's gift to Big D. The science of geophysics was his special knowledge. His Swedish immigrant parents created the home in which his honest, strong, and charitable character was created. He had led the technology effort which developed military contracts in WWII. Those contracts funded research that ultimately created the heart of today's iPhone, the microchip.

One of Jonsson's big projects was "Goals for Dallas." His 1960 efforts affirmed the town's growth and cultural character and targeted how to do it in the future. Wyly and Johnson worked with other local leaders to help Dallas grow in education, culture, technology and economic results to make this a good place to live.

At the opening of the company's Tulsa office, UCC employee number three, Ross Rumore (far left), and first investor, Ben Voth (second from right), stand by while Sam greets local dignitaries, including the governor of Oklahoma, Henry Bellman (center).

Below: Wyly's red 1966 Mustang is parked outside the UCC building.

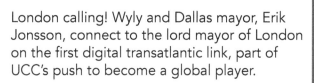

London calling! Wyly and Dallas mayor, Erik Jonsson, connect to the lord mayor of London on the first digital transatlantic link, part of UCC's push to become a global player.

THE BIRTH OF THE INTERNET

Tulsa was the first expansion because it too had a lot of petroleum engineers needing computer power to solve complex geological problems, such as how to pump the oil from underneath Long Beach, California, without the city sinking into the sea.

Wyly created the term "computer utility" to describe the marriage of the telephone and the computer, the happy union that would change the world.

The typewriter evolved into the keyboard of personal computers and the smartphones, iPhones, iPads, and other digital devices today. In the early days, the invention of the typewriter impacted the economy, changed families, and opened up new jobs for women as clerks and secretaries.

Fortune editor, Gene Bylinsky, wrote in 1976, "Sam Wyly, an engaging and boyish-looking computer technology pioneer, introduced the concept of a 'computer utility' and built his successful University Computing headquarters in Dallas. He is now creating another pioneering concern, Data Transmission Company, a telephone company for computers. Until Wyly came along with Datran, computers were forced to communicate in a costly and convoluted way over old-fashioned telephone wires designed for the human voice. As Wyly told a cheering national conference, 'The computer industry has dialed into a busy signal.'"

The internet was born after we married the telephone and the computer—chips got cheaper.

Sterling Commerce was sold to AT&T for $4 billion in 2000 as the "phone company" was trying to become a "computer company" too.

Ed Whitacre from Ennis did two main things. He moved AT&T to Dallas and took the call from Steve Jobs when Jobs needed a partnership in creating the iPhone.

August 28, 2017

Mr. Sam Wyly
300 Crescent Court, Suite 850
Dallas, TX 75201

Dear Sam,

Thank you so very much for the wonderful book, *Legacy, the journey of German-Jews*. And I noticed that it was autographed by the author, Werner Frank.

The note is inscribed: "To my mentor." I assumed that is you, until I read further, and assured myself that it was indeed you!

I'll enjoy reading it.

My mother lost most of her family during the holocaust: her grandparents, aunts, uncles and cousins. Her parents escaped Strasbourg/Alsace Lorraine as Hitler was invading it.

Last April, Laura, son Max, and I flew to Krakow to visit Auschwitz-Birkenau. It was an extraordinary visit.

I hope you are well. I saw your children in Aspen last month and we had a nice visit. We're off to La Jolla this coming week to escape the Texas heat. I'll call you when we return so we can get together.

With kind regards,

Steven D. Wolens

STEVE WOLENS AND LAURA MILLER

Steve Wolens is a former Texas State Representative married to Laura Miller. Laura Miller was born in Baltimore and educated in Madison, Wisconsin, and a journalist in Miami and Dallas. She was Mayor of Dallas from 2002-2007.

Steve Wolens' mother escaped Strasburg through the south of France just before the Nazi tank invasion in 1939. She escaped to America through the South of France to East Texas.

Wolens led the Texas house when George W. Bush was governor. Together, they got electricity deregulation done right in Texas when California and northeastern states could not.

Much of the gas production in West Texas today is being pipelined to the Texas Gulf Coast and sold in China and other Asian nations through the Panama Canal. New technologies developed here underlay this huge USA success. Texas now leads the United States in oil and gas production, wind and solar power production and air pollution has dramatically decreased and air quality improved.

CLEAN AIR THROUGH CLEAN ENERGY

Major North American Electrical Grids

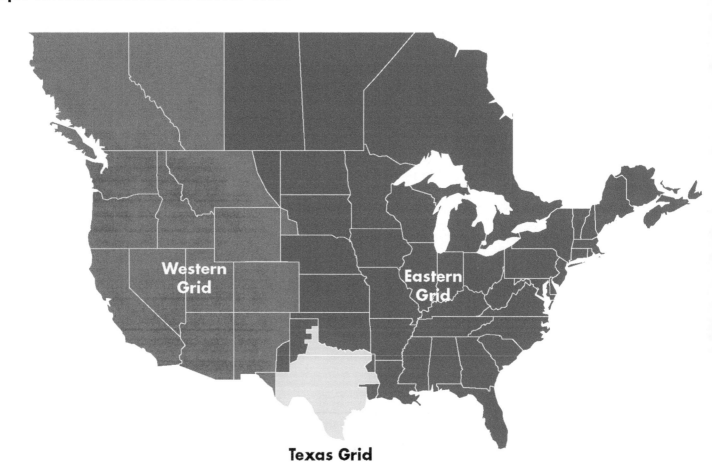

Western Grid

Eastern Grid

Texas Grid

BURGER CAPITAL OF AMERICA

Texas is home to several burger restaurants, including What-a-Burger, Texas Burger and Twisted Root as well as elegant restaurants that serve five-star burgers! Although there's an ongoing debate as to what the best burger on the planet truly is, we can safely say that Texas is the best burger capital of America!

Dallas created the corn chip ("Fritos" is the generic name) while Herman Lay in Georgia had created the potato chip.

So, a merger became Frito Lay headquartered in Big D—first at Exchange Park on Harry Hines and then in Plano. Later, PepsiCo was added. And the "Cola Wars" of TV ads began with the Taste Test, "Can you tell which is which? Coca Cola or Pepsi Cola?"

Later, when Apple's board fired Steve Jobs as CEO, they recruited the head of Pepsi from Dallas: John Sculley. It was a disastrous decision. Potato chips ain't computer chips!

And Fritos and potato chips and Pepsi rolled on.

DALLAS ENTREPRENEURSHIP

Dallas is an entrepreneurial town—home to game-changers.

It has many city councils, county governments, school boards, school teachers, churches, civic groups, and neighborhoods that are vastly inclusive and free for individuals and families.

It's is an innovative mixture of entrepreneurs from all over the world. What is an entrepreneur? The tech startup, flower shop or art gallery owner, the land developer, Real Estate professional, vendor at the Farmers Market, and the multimillion dollar print shop. Dallas got it right, by creating an atmosphere of growth, learning, and education where entrepreneurs thrive. In North Texas there are hundreds of entrepreneur think tanks, clubs, masterminds, and resources for both the savvy and startup entrepreneur.

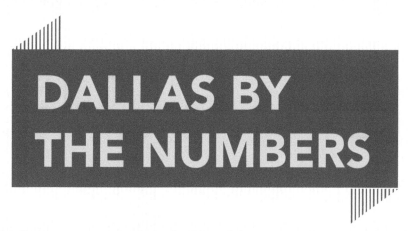

DALLAS BY THE NUMBERS

Frisco is the fastest growing town in the United States.

When Sam Wyly first arrived, Dallas was the sixteenth largest city in the United States; now it is the fourth largest metro area.

Dallas is the fastest growing city in the United States.

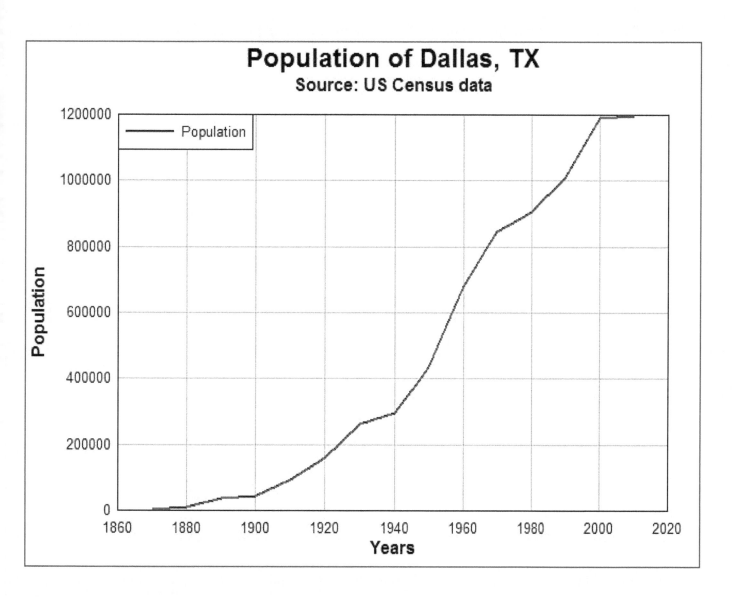

BETTE NESMITH GRAHAM

Bette Nesmith Graham lived in Richardson and worked at Texas Bank and Trust. Bette invented Paint Out in her kitchen with tempera water-based paint, and used it at work for five years with improvements from her son's chemistry teacher at Thomas Jefferson High School. Coworkers often sought Bette's "paint out."

The name was changed to Liquid Paper. Bette ran her company with a combination of spirituality, egalitarianism, and pragmatism. Her faith in Christian Science inspired the development of her corporate emphasis on product quality over profit motive. She believed women brought a more nurturing and humanistic quality to the male world of business.

In 1979, she sold Liquid Paper for $47.5 million, ($160 million 2017 money.)

Her son, Michael Nesmith, gained fame in American rock and pop band, The Monkees.

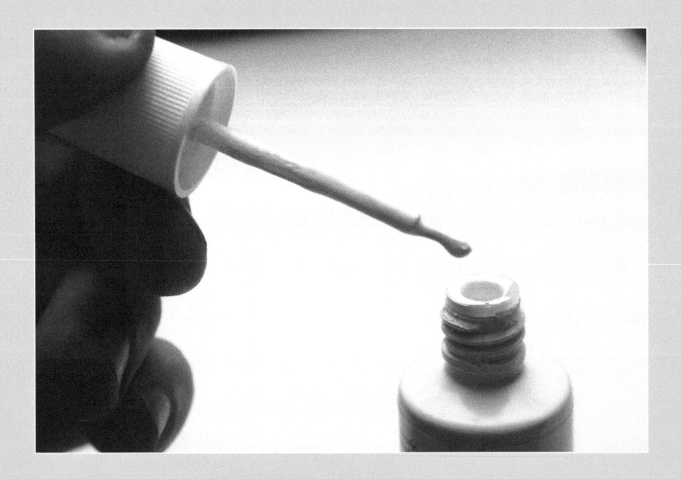

THE AIRLINE INDUSTRY

Braniff

Oklahoma-based Braniff moved operations to Love Field in 1934 after the USPS awarded it an airmail route between Dallas and Chicago.

Later it was run by a CEO named Lawrence who married a Madison Avenue advertising executive named Mary Wells.

They repainted the Braniff jets in vibrant colors— the "End of the plain plane."

American Airlines

American Airlines is headquartered in Dallas, Texas, and several executives, flight attendants, and global pilots are trained here. With a vast network of aircraft and thousands of employees, American flies to almost every city in the country, and all over the world.

Evan flies to Rapid City, SD and drives to Spearfish, SD—a Dakota drive no further than DFW to Garland.

MARK CUBAN

If you were to ask what entrepreneur in the last 20 years has had the most successful exit in Dallas, most folks would say, "Mark Cuban!" In 1999, Mark Cuban sold his company, Broadcast.com, to Yahoo! for $5.7 billion.

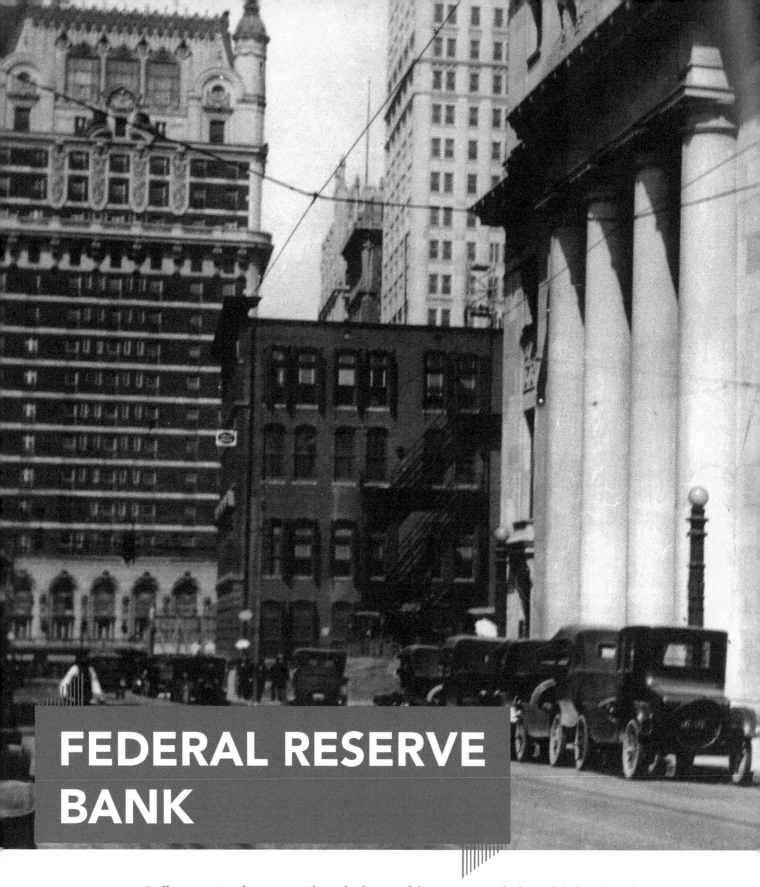

FEDERAL RESERVE BANK

Dallas won its placement. It's in the heart of downtown with the Adolphus Hotel and the Magnolia building. Around the corner was First National Bank which morphed into the "Tall Green One" on the cover of this book. In the '60s and '70s Sam was their youngest director.

A GOOD PLACE FOR SENIORS

Seniors from across the country and the world move to Dallas, whether it's for a trailer house or a million-dollar condo.

HOUSING MARKET

A house is lower in cost in Greater Dallas than in New York or California whether it's a small home in the suburb, a trailer park home, or a million-dollar condominium. Electricity is half the cost of electricity in Manhattan. New York governments have banned fracking (which Texas loves), which makes "the rents too high," a common reason to move out.

In the Dallas area, mini mansions abound, and an incredibly affordable lifestyle, home, and yard can be attained easily. In various parts of uptown and downtown as well as out-lying areas there are old warehouses and lofts converted to apartments, vintage spaces, and modern high rises.

ONE RIOT-ONE RANGER

Texas Rangers

Laurie and David visited the Texas Rangers' Museum in Waco.

Frank Hamer led the Texas Rangers who shot Bonnie and Clyde near Louisiana Tech in the 1930s.

Sam saw Bonnie and Clyde's bullet-riddled car at the state fair in Shreveport when I was in high school.

Later, the stories about them being from Oak Cliff were in Goff's Hamburgers located across from SMU for decades. Their story was often retold by Dallas developer Trammel Crow.

When local "rednecks and bullies" were rioting, Dallas' mayor called Waco for help—expecting a big crew of Rangers on the train.

When only Ranger got off, the mayor asked, "Where's more Rangers?"

Answer: "You got one riot. You got one Ranger."

That's all that was needed.

MILITARY MUSCLE

Texas has a long and colorful history when it comes to the United Sates military. Besides the many sons and daughters who have served in all of the military branches, Texas has built ships, tanks, and planes and produced oil and gas to fuel all of the above.

Big Organizations and Military

1940 to 1960 was the Age of Big Organizations. There were big corporations for mass production of ships, trucks, tanks, airplanes, and big projects as air fields and the Big Inch Pipeline on the "Home Front."

A big Army and big Navy (each with their own airplanes then), to win the wars on both fronts. Oklahoma, Louisiana, and Texas produced most of America's oil and gas in World War II and still do.

The Lone Star state produced 40 percent of US oil and 25 percent of the world's oil, with a refining capacity of about the same. Construction on the pipeline began when German U-boats began sinking tankers in the Gulf of Mexico.

FDR during the Great Depression years when one of three were out of work in the USA and many federal "pump priming projects" built infrastructure.

Our World War II Heroes

"Dorie" Miller was born and raised on a farm near Waco. After war began in Europe in September 1939, nineteen-year-old Dorie enlisted in the US Navy and was assigned to Pearl Harbor. On Sunday, December 7, 1941, Dorie's fighting instincts would be turned against attackers from the sky.

Texas was the training center for the Women's Airforce Service Pilots (WASP). Avenger Field in Sweetwater was the only all-female training base in the United States.

Sam Dealey was the most decorated sailor of World War II. He graduated from Oak Cliff High School.

Dealey commanded the submarine USS *Harder* and led six war patrols in 1943 and 1944.

Audie Murphy was born into a large sharecropper family in Hunt County, near Greenville, TX and became the most decorated combat soldiers of World War II.

Rusty Hays, my friend at Third Church, parachuted into Normandy in the D-Day invasion and fought house to house with his fellow troops all the way until the Nazi surrender. Like most guys who came home from this tough duty, he never talked about it, but Rusty wrote a day-by-day, house-by-house, mile-to-mile account of his dangerous duty on through VE Day, and Rusty's son, Bill, gave me a copy.

Dorie Miller

Sam Dealey

Audie Murphy

Louisiana Military Maneuvers of 1941

Of America's Army of one-million men, 500,000 were involved in the maneuvers. Maneuvers tested troops in the bayous and piney woods with a competitive "Blue Army" versus a "Red Army" in terrain from Lake Charles up to Shreveport.

Hitler had invaded Russia after conquering France and daily bombing of Britain. America was getting ready to go "over there" for a war in Europe.

Lots of Sam's uncles and cousins and men in the neighborhood would be going. Cousin Jane would be waiting for her "Beau," Heiman Cohn.

At boot camp, the drill sergeant hollers you awake while abruptly turning night into day with bright barracks lights, gives you 2 minutes to have your boots on and be standing at attention in company formation to march to the mess hall for breakfast. Then he marches you 20 miles a day. An overeducated MBA just out of University of Michigan grad school learns to love his sturdy boots.

"When I came to work in Dallas after college and military duty, it seemed that, like me, everybody else was from somewhere else too."

Sam at boot camp at Lackland Air Force Base in San Antonio, where the boot camp sergeant was in "hurry up" mode on spelling "Wyly."

America's Vital Military Muscle

Lockheed Aircraft Plant in Grand Prairie has 20,000 well-paid workers who build fighter bombers to help America keep the world more free. It is next door to the Joint Air Force Military Base. Hurst, north of Fort Worth, which has the Bell Helicopter plant. We make airplanes and fly them out of Dyess AFB in Abilene, Texas or Barksdale AFB in Bossier Parish in Louisiana. White Sands Proving Ground in NM, an extension of Fort Bliss, is where we tested the atomic bomb and the Tomahawk missiles (verified by Col. Jim). They do tank maneuvers there, too. Fort Bliss in El Paso, TX is almost a million acres, the world's largest.

THE AMERICAN CHALLENGE

This was how Europe saw the USA in the 1960s. "The American Challenge is not ruthless like so many Europe has known in her history," wrote Frenchman, John Servan-Schriener in 1967.

After the war, America produced 50% of the world's economic goods and services. France feared the coming competition from American companies in Europe.

US Army troops had carried the Coca Cola brand with them during the war in Europe and Asia.

But the Marshall Plan paid for rebuilding Germany and other European nations in the late 1940s and early 1950s.

Ditto for Japan. Most victors throughout history had demanded reparations from the conquered. The United States sends dollars and knew how to build free market democracies. This is still true today. Without America, the world would be less free and less prosperous.

America remains the one indispensable nation.

NEW ORLEANS SHIPYARDS

Navy destroyer USS *Edward Sparrow,* named for our granddad born in Ireland in 1810, was launched in New Orleans shipyards in 1940s. Sam's Uncle William Evans (Flora's brother) worked as a welder there.

Ladies smashed bottles of champagne on the ship bow for good luck in the movie news reels we saw at the movie every Saturday in Lake Providence during World War II.

Two of Granddad Evans' sisters lived in the Pontalba Apartments on Jackson Square. One was society editor of the *Times Picayune* newspaper.

SOLDIERS

Soldiers coming through DFW are headed either to Ft. Hood in San Antonio or Ft. Bliss in El Paso.

IKE

General Eisenhower was born in Denison in Grayson County.

    His dad worked for Katy Railroad in Denison from 1888 to 1892, and his father's family were prosperous Mennonite Kansas farmers as they had been in Pennsylvania and Germany. After four years in Texas, Ike grew up back in mid-Kansas.

    His mom's German ancestors came to Kansas from the Shenandoah Valley of Virginia.

FAMILIES AND DIVERSITY

Dallas, as well as Texas as a whole, has been called home by a number of families. Perhaps one of the most notable families of recent history would be the Bush family, two of whom are former presidents of the United States.

Dallas has been the new home of choice for many people, and one reason for that is the diverse cultures that are so well represented across the city and the state. There are thousands of people with different heritages, religious beliefs, and views all living together in a rapidly growing city.

THANKSGIVING SQUARE

Freedom of religion is a constitutionally protected right, which has made America the number one global destination for Christian migrants, as well as Buddhists and those who declare no religious affiliation. 74 percent of the foreign-born population is Christian, and about five percent is Muslim. The United States is also a leading destination for Jewish and Hindu migrants.

When we talk about Spanish missions in Texas, the very first missions were in the piney woods of East Texas.

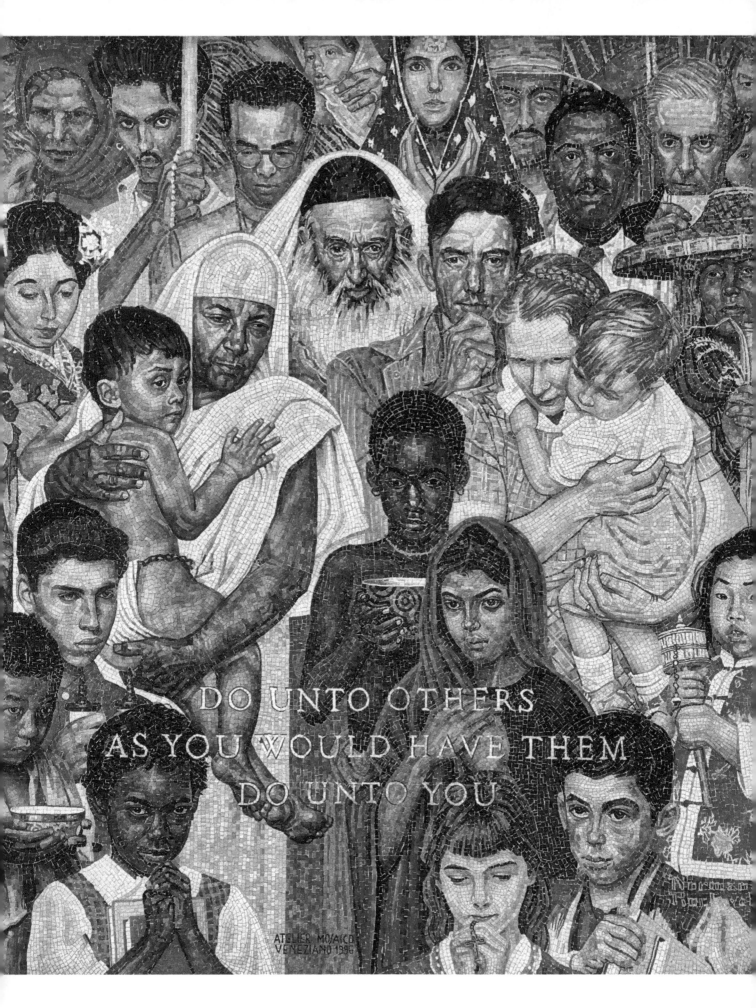

CHURCHES

St. Patrick's Cathedral in Fort Worth was designed in the popular Gothic Revival. Magnificent details include a large stained-glass window above the main entrance.

In downtown Dallas, a heavily Irish congregation shifted to mostly Latino, and the church was renamed "Cathedral Shrine of the Virgin of Guadalupe."

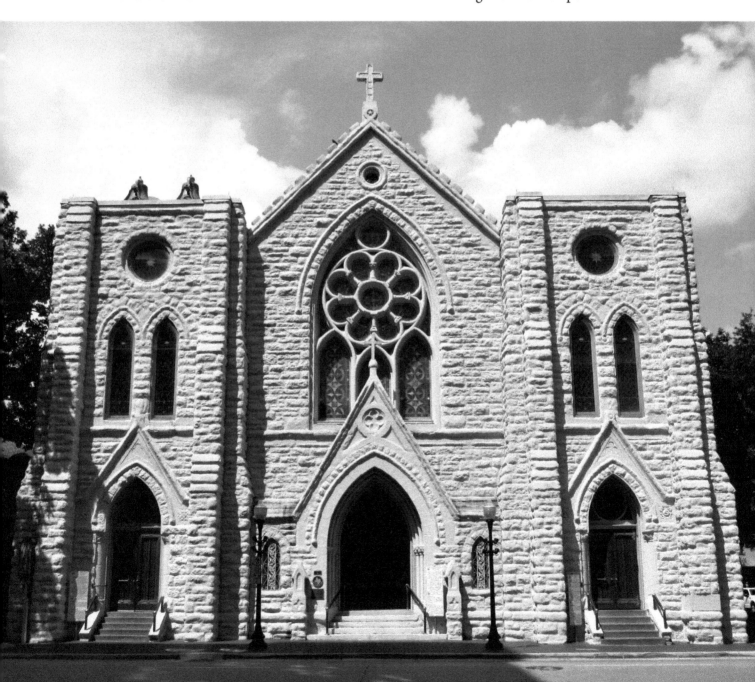

GIVING BACK

GOD IS LOVE
1 John

Lakewood Church

Throughout the years, the area has had a reputation of giving with more than 30,000 ministries sprouting up, to help people in need. Whether it's a hospital, or to help early childhood education, serve meals to the homeless, fight heart disease, or support autism, this is an area overflowing with servant leaders eager to meet needs.

Churches in Dallas today are comprised of many different names and congregations, and trace their roots back to circuit riding preachers and teachers and backwoods revivals inspired by Tennessee Presbyterians. There are houses of worship dotting every town and suburb, churches that appeal to millennials in downtown industrial buildings, open-air homeless churches and cowboy churches in buildings and country fields. Several of the churches planted all over the world have originated in and are connected to Dallas.

Oaklawn Church

DALLAS CARES

The people of Dallas help each other, continually giving back to the community. Heroic Texans help others in crisis. Whether it's flood or hurricane relief, a dog shelter, helping the homeless or serving at one of the local battered women's shelters, Dallas charities are a big part of the community. The first charity was formed by local women to care for wounded and crippled veterans stumbling home from the Civil War. It is all about bringing people together; people speak to each other.

Dallas is a town strong on family values and hospitality. All roads lead to Dallas, and greater Dallas is far and wide, encompassing so many more cities than can be listed. When Sam was in New York, he was amazed at the difference. Walking down Manhattan avenues where no one spoke to anyone, except for taxi drivers hollering at each other. Culture shock! But, as he got to know some locals there—he met lots of kind and friendly folk—all within their more contained neighborhood places.

BUSH FAMILY

George H. W. Bush

Like many Americans, the Bush family goes back to Europeans seeking freedom from religious oppression.

After graduating high school in 1942, George H. W. Bush joined the Navy and became a pilot at age 18. He trained in Texas at Corpus Christi. As of June 9, 1943, he was the youngest pilot. In WWII, after taking off from an aircraft carrier, his plane was shot down. Years later, the USS *George H. W. Bush* aircraft carrier was named in his honor and keeps the peace.

President Bush once said, "The Wylys backed me in every race I ever ran, and never asked for anything."

The George Bush Presidential Library is at Texas A&M University. Forty-nine percent of its grads were in WWI, and over 20,000 combat troops in WWI—with more officers than West Point and Annapolis combined. It has over 50,000 students today.

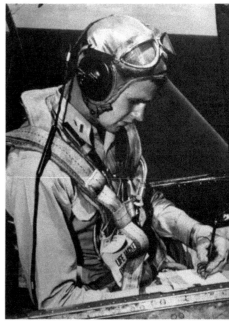

George W. Bush

When George H. W. Bush and Barbara came to Midland after Navy service and Yale, he named his off-shore drilling company Zapata.

His son, George W. Bush was asked, "What's the difference between you and your dad"?

"He went to the New England Country Day School and I went to Midland Junior High."

Both are Yale grads. Both landed their planes on air-craft carriers; dad during World War II. On immigration, "W" said, "We're a nation of laws, and we must enforce our laws. We're also a nation of immigrants, and we must uphold that tradition, which has strengthened our country in so many ways."

Like Winston Churchill did earlier after winning wars to save democracy and freedom in the world, President George W. Bush took up painting.

George Prescott Bush

Texas Land Commissioner Bush is a fourth-generation elected official of the Bush family, grandson of President George H. W. Bush, the son of former Florida Governor Jeb Bush, nephew of President George W. Bush, and great-grandson of Prescott Bush, senator from Connecticut during the Eisenhower years, and a golfing buddy of "Ike."

Commissioner Bush dedicated his life to public service—working as a public schoolteacher after Rice University, serving in Afghanistan as a Navy officer, and the 28th Land Commissioner, the only state agency that makes more money than it spends.

Born in Houston, he worked in Fort Worth and now lives with his family in Austin.

SPORTS, COMMERCE, AND TRAILBLAZERS

Dallas is home to a variety of sports teams, business ventures, and individuals blazing their own trails. From professional athletes to entrepreneurs, the city is alive with the spirit of adventure and offers an unparalleled business-friendly atmosphere.

DALLAS FOOTBALL

John Stephen Jones led Highland Park High School to the state championship two years in a row, 2016 and 2017. Three generations of the Jones family saw the game at Cowboy Stadium. Other HP quarterbacks include Matthew Stafford and Bobby Lane.

Lance McIlhenny was the winningest quarterback at SMU and in Southwest Conference history. When Evan was a "Gold Eagle" from Armstrong, Lance was a "White Wildcat" from Hyer. Both went to McCullough Middle School and Highland Park High School.

They were on the road to a state championship—until Odessa Permian came to town with a West Texas crowd that filled the stadium with their ear-shattering "Mojo! Mojo!" They inspired the *Friday Night Lights* movie and TV series.

Doak Walker was earlier. He won a Super Bowl for Detroit.

Dak Prescott (Mississippi State Bulldogs) from Haughton High School in Bossier Parish, Louisiana, won 13 games for the Dallas Cowboys as a rookie quarterback—an NFL record breaker.

Bob Lilly of Texas Christian University was the first draft pick ever of the Dallas Cowboys.

Roger Staubach played in 1963 Cotton Bowl—Navy vs. SMU—and was Heisman Trophy winner. He led the Cowboys to five Super Bowls. Maryanne and Roger make the Army/Navy game every year. The 2016 winner played Louisiana Tech in the Armed Forces Bowl at TCU Stadium (Tech 48; Navy 45).

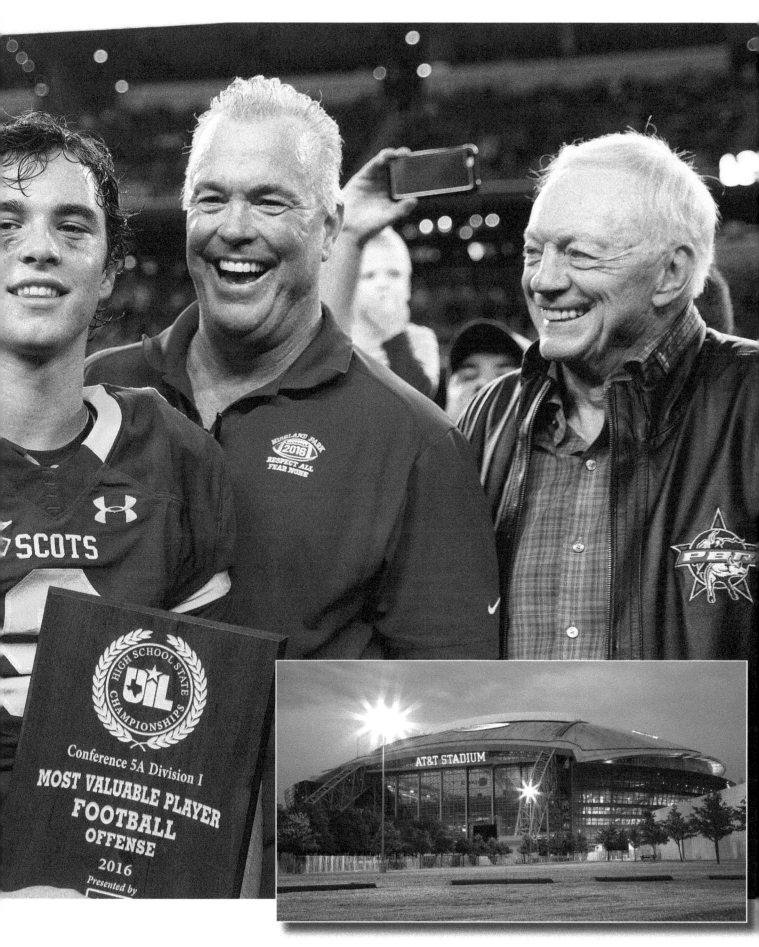

DOAK WALKER—WON A "SUPER BOWL" FOR DETROIT LIONS

Doak Walker graduated from Highland Park High School and SMU, joined the US Army, and was a Heisman Trophy winner.

Sam listened on the radio at his town in Louisiana to the SMU/Notre Dame football games in 1948 and 1949.

The name, "Super Bowl," came later from Lamar Hunt, who created the name from watching his kids play with a "super ball."

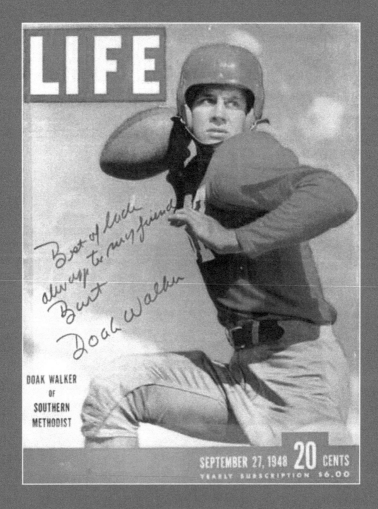

LAMAR HUNT

Lamar is the true founder of the NFL as we know it. His Kansas City Chiefs were originally the Dallas Texans.

FIRST GAME
CHIEFS - 13
COWBOYS - 0
AT COTTON BOWL
SEPT 5, 1970

HIGHLAND PARK GRADE SCHOOL FOOTBALL

When Sam's children were little, we had Armstrong, Bradfield, Hyer, and University Park elementary schools.

Hyer's Lance McIlhenny, quarterbacked for SMU, and led the Mustangs two SWC Championships in 1981 and 1982. He was a "White Wildcat" at Hyer.

Highland Park is the best public high school in the State of Texas—for many decades almost 100 percent of its grads have gone on to college.

Two Highland Park boys were the highest paid NFL and MLB athletes in 2017—Matthew Stafford and Clayton Kershaw. They were the "Blue Bruisers" of Bradfield.

Frisco is the fastest growing town in America, named for a stop on the San Francisco railroad. In addition to many company headquarters, Frisco is home to the Texas Legends basketball team, the Dallas Stars, FC Dallas soccer, and the Frisco Rough Riders. The Dallas Cowboys, "America's Team," recently moved its headquarters and practice field to Frisco.

The Bob Rowling family came to Big D from Corpus Christi. They partnered with the Jerry Jones family on the 16-story Omni Frisco Hotel—named Star. Speaking of his parents and grandparents, Bob said, "The first million is the hardest."

Evan Wyly is a founder of the Texas Legends, an NBA minor league team. Evan was excited to start a new professional basketball team in Frisco with his friend Donnie Nelson, GM of the Dallas Mavericks. It's rewarding to help young players and staff develop and move on to the NBA. Frisco is a fantastic home for the team, and the community support enables the team to set league records for attendance. Giving back to the community is important, and each home game focuses on a different local charity, who gets to design the jersey for the game. Evan and Donnie are happy that Mark Cuban has recently joined them as majority owner.

FRISCO

DALLAS GOT IT RIGHT!

BASKETBALL

Dirk Nowitzki

Dirk Nowitzki, who came to the Dallas Mavericks from Germany, recently became the sixth NBA player to score 30,000 points in his career.

Karl Malone

Karl Malone, a graduate of Louisiana Tech, made the 30,000 Point Club and lives in Ruston, Louisiana off Highway 80 on the road to Sam Wyly's high school town of Delhi, where Sam's dad was editor and publisher of *The Delhi Dispatch*, who was the chosen as a Democratic candidate for the electoral college, but he resigned in order to editorialize for General Dwight Eisenhower.

GOLFERS

Jordan Spieth was born in Dallas in 1993. His first major win came in the 2015 Masters Tournament.

Lee Trevino was born in Dallas of Mexican ancestry. His uncle introduced him to golf with a few golf balls and an old club. Trevino won six major championships and 29 PGA Tour events.

KAUFMAN RANCH

Toddie Lee Wynne led "the Texas Oil guys" in the battle in the "hot oil wars" in east Texas (a battle for free markets against federal regulation and control). He was a neighbor in Highland Park, and built the Hong Kong Hilton Hotel. His brother, Angus, started "Six Flags Over Texas."

Toddie Lee Wynne's Star Brand Ranch in Kaufman County hosted the first Cattle Baron's Ball.

JUANITA MARTINEZ

Juanita Martinez was the first Latina on Dallas City Council. She was very active in the arts. Her family built the first El Fenix restaurant in 1918 in downtown Dallas. It is the oldest chain of Mexican restaurants in the United States.

VOTE APRIL 6

CITY COUNCIL
PLACE 9

MRS. ALFRED (ANITA)
Martinez

Your partner for a better life

A tireless civic worker, Anita Martinez has demonstrated a special concern for Dallas' young people. She is seeking a second City Council term. She is a charter director, National Center for Voluntary Action; director, Dallas YWCA; member, General Council, Dallas Young Adult Institute, and member, Criminal Justice Council, North Central Texas Council of Governments. She is a "Goals for Dallas" conferee and twice has been cited as one of Dallas' most oustanding women and newsmakers. Keep her working as your partner for a better life. Re-elect Anita Martinez April 6.

MRS. ANITA MARTIN
COUNCILWOMAN

LUCCHESE BOOTS

Cowboy boots are the reigning symbol of Texas culture for a good reason: cowboy boots are how we tell the world we're Texan, and how we express ourselves.

Walk into almost any boot store in the state and you'll see hundreds if not thousands of designs and patterns and styles. And, if you don't see something you like, a custom boot maker will craft a pair just for you.

The father of custom bootmaking was a Sicilian named Salvatore Lucchese, who came from Italy to San Antonio in 1882.

Lucchese and his sons and grandsons have made boots by hand in their El Paso workshop for everyone from Teddy Roosevelt to LBJ to Francisco Madero, the leader of the revolution that brought democracy to Mexico in the early 20th century.

Lucchese released 125 pairs of special boots that retailed for $12,500, to celebrate its 125th anniversary.

BOY SCOUTS

Sam and Charles Wyly were cub scouts who collected tin cans to be melted down for ships and tanks for our troops, like today's kids do in the White Rock Lake neighborhood of Dallas. The Scout Master, Frank Lawrence, was a Rice University grad and a petroleum engineer for Sun Oil.

The Boy Scouts, headquartered in Dallas, have 2.4 million participants and a million adult volunteers.

Pictured here are Sam and Charles getting Eagle Scout badges from their mom and dad in Delhi, Louisiana. Scoutmaster Frank Lawrence, a Sun Oil Petroleum engineer out of Rice University, took Sam's troop to join 48,000 scouts at the world jamboree in Valley Forge, Pennsylvania. General Eisenhower and President Truman came to speak.

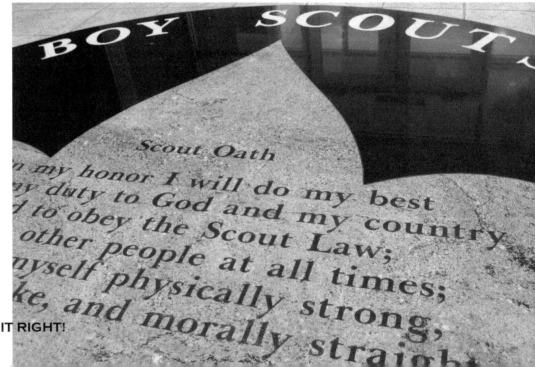

HIGHLAND PARK

Highland Park Pharmacy is a soda fountain place where you can get a pimento cheese sandwich on Knox Street. The Knox railroad station was five miles north of Dallas's Union Station and the first stop on the Katy headed North and East. For decades, local college kids rode off and returned home from school on the train.

"THE DOG LIFT" FROM HILLSBORO TO ASPEN

Rescue dogs from Hillsboro, Texas to Aspen, Colorado flew on the Wyly Gulfstream jet for adoption at the Cheryl and Sam Wyly Animal shelter in Aspen, Colorado.

Rescuing dogs and an overall love for animals is a way of life. Seth Sachson, who runs the Aspen Animal Shelter, is a graduate of St. Mark's School in North Dallas. He has a program where people can invite a dog out for the day to join in a hike. At every Saturday market, Seth has several dogs, and local parents and kids looking for a pet. Seth does such a great job that some at the Saturday market who did not know they needed a pet dog, adopt one!

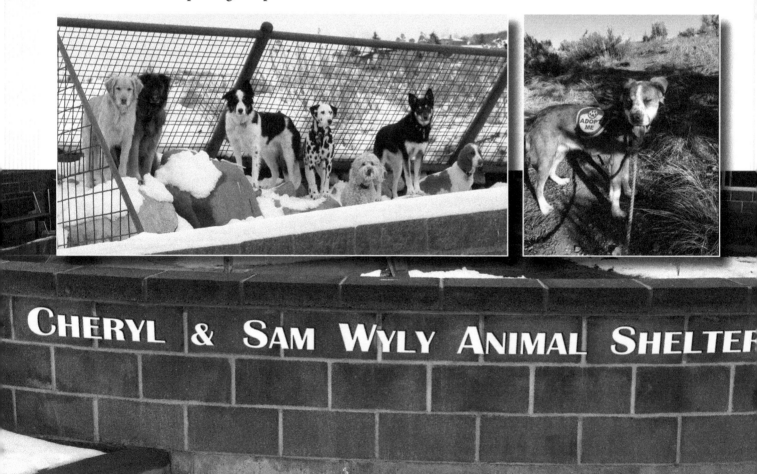

FORT WORTH

Fort Worth Stock Exchange bought and sold cows, not corporate stocks or bonds.

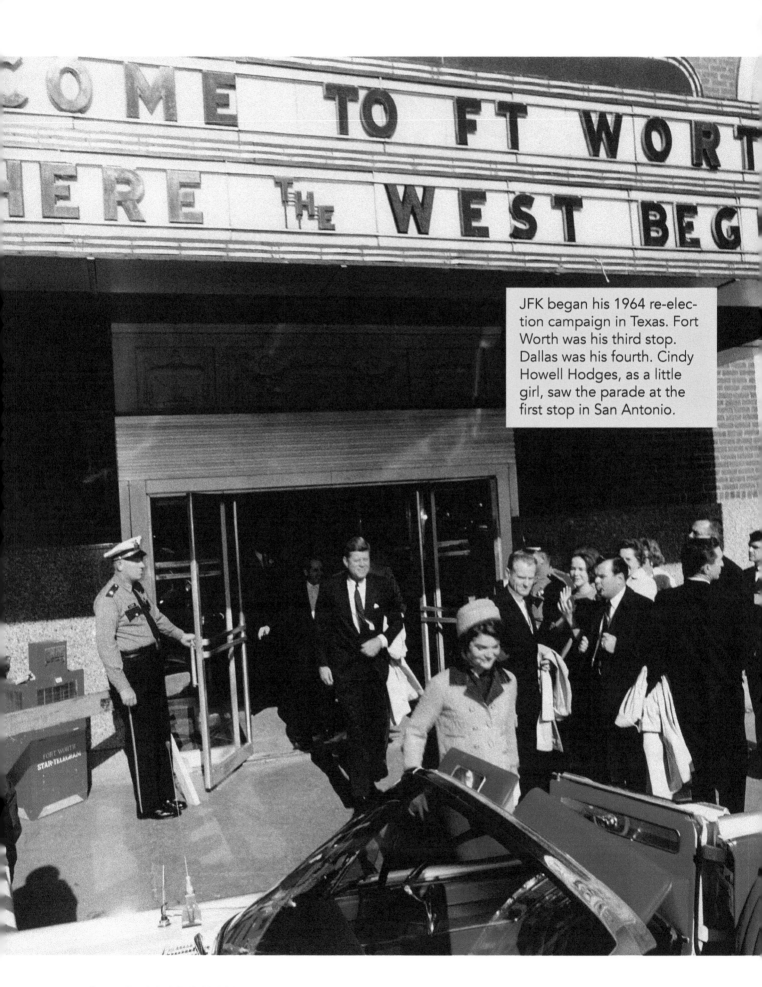

JFK began his 1964 re-election campaign in Texas. Fort Worth was his third stop. Dallas was his fourth. Cindy Howell Hodges, as a little girl, saw the parade at the first stop in San Antonio.

SOUTHERN STAR

Allie Beth Allman

From humble beginnings on a North Texas Farm, Allie Beth Allman found success as the go-to realtor for Dallas. The free-spirited, blonde-haired, blue-eyed girl knew how to milk a cow and harvest wheat, and could walk barefoot two miles into the North Texas town.

And when she wasn't at school or taking ballet lessons, she was sitting at the dinner table with her two sisters, her father, and her mother eating her mothers' freshly made fried chicken, rolls, and ice cream. She didn't understand money—or that her family didn't have much of it—and she couldn't read a word due to dyslexia. But in her mind, she was rich and the world was at her feet. "There's plenty of room in this town for everyone to succeed," she says about a life lesson she learned when she was young. "My parents never said you do anything. They said you will."

Whatever the reason, Allie Beth Allman (née Allie Beth McMurtry) grew up thinking she could do anything. So she built a Dallas residential real estate empire.

-quoted from Danielle Abril of *D Magazine*

POSSUM KINGDOM

PRESIDENTIAL SPEECHWRITER

Karen Hughes was born in Paris, France, to a US diplomat family. Her dad was the last US governor of the Panama Canal.

After graduating from W. T. White High School, Hughes earned a bachelor's degree at SMU.

Mary Matalin talks with Karen Hughes and Lynne Cheney in the President's Emergency Operations Center.

"IRON LADY"
MARGARET THATCHER

She led the change in Britain from a mostly socialist state to a market democracy. She and George H. W. Bush were addressing the Aspen Institute when Saddam Hussein of Iraq grabbed Kuwait. President Bush said, "You have until January 15th to get out or we will throw you out." Thatcher backed the USA as 500,000 American troops and their allies removed this petty dictator who had used germ warfare on his own Kurdish people. Her family lives in Dallas.

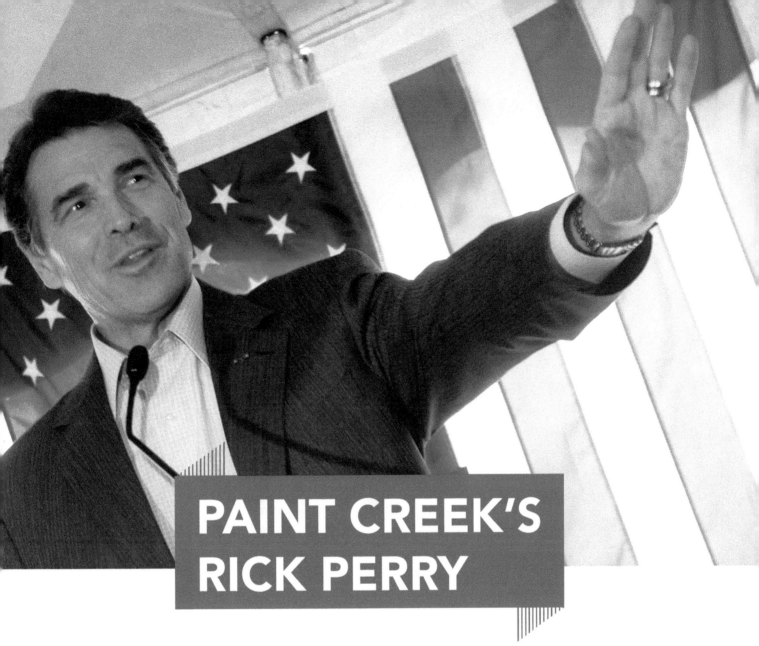

PAINT CREEK'S RICK PERRY

Rich Perry is a 5th generation Texan from Haskell and Paint Creek, Texas and a graduate of A&M in animal science. Following service at Dyess Air Force Base in Abilene, elected as a Democrat to the State House and one of the "Pit Bulls" who pushed for limited government spending, then Commissioner of Agriculture. He switched to the Republican party when most Texans felt that the national Democratic party had left them for the east and west coast liberals.

As Texas leads the nation in oil and gas and wind and solar energy production, he now serves as US Secretary of Energy. He was governor of Texas (for 14 years— longest serving governor). Rick gave Sam a history paper written by his grandfather in 1926 of his battle-by-battle service in a Texas company during the Civil War, which was very similar to the service record of his own great-grandfather Irwin's with a Mississippi Company.

GOVERNOR BILL CLEMENTS

Bill Clements became the first Republican governor of Texas after the 100 post-Civil War years, when Texas was changing from being a loyal part of the "Democratic Solid South."

Governor Clements called James Michener, after he had published his great historical novel, *Centennial*. Colorado joined the United States in 1876—our nation's 100th birthday and asked, "What will it take to do a similar historical Texas?" The author was surprised and pleased when Clements got him what he wanted, and more, at UT Austin. As an entrepreneur, Bill Clements built a highly successful oil drilling company.

To Sam Wyly
With best wishes
Bill Clements

Clements' wife Rita and Sam were earlier the two delegates to the convention that nominated Nixon for president—both selected by Peter O'Donnell who built the Texas Republican Party from nothing in the '60s and '70s when the Eastern and West Coast and Northeast states were taking control of the Democratic Party from the South and Mountain states of the West.

Born in Wichita Falls; raised in Longview and Duncanville. Wife, Cecilia Phalen Abbott, first Latina First Lady.

GOVERNOR GREG ABBOTT

From Oak Cliff—Bonnie & Clyde 1930s bank robbers

DALLAS THUGS

COKESBURY BOOKSTORE

Cokesbury Bookstore was the big downtown bookstore of the '40s, '50s, '60s, '70s, and '80s.

Book publishers would want their authors to do book signings at Cokesbury Bookstore in Dallas. Then stores followed to suburbia. Now high-rises are too expensive.

Sharon Andersen and family have a Half Price Books store on Northwest Highway. Memphis, Tennessee has Burks, Juggler, Two Rivers, Barnes & Noble, and Book Place.

Interabang Books is a 5,000 foot bookstore located in Preston Royal. For a number of years, the independent bookstores were in decline because of the digital world. That's stopped. Both print and digital are big markets worldwide for English-language books. The first or second language of business worldwide is English.

Nancy Perot is an investor. Her dad Ross Perot ran for president of the United States against both the Democratic nominee, (Bill Clinton of Arkansas), and the Republican (George H. W. Bush). Perot got more votes than any third candidate since Teddy Roosevelt in 1912. Nancy's mom Margot Perot built the maternity hospital at Presbyterian in Northeast Dallas.

MISSISSIPPI RIVER DELTA

The book *Unconquered* is a saga of Jerry Lee Lewis, rock piano player; Jimmy Swaggart, TV and Baton Rouge preacher; and Mickey Gilley the country music star. Like Elvis Presley, who was born in Tupelo, Mississippi, in the Delta part of the Mississippi River, these three Ferriday, Louisiana boys were dirt poor and learned music and song plus preaching in an Assembly of God Church. The Ferriday church was actually organized by a lady missionary from Dallas.

Mississippi means, "Father of waters" in its Indian name. It drains the middle of America from Pittsburgh to the Yellowstone in the mountainous West. The Mississippi River below Cairo, Illinois, dumps into the ocean is the Delta. It includes towns on both sides of the river. It was the rich cotton land. You had big plantations and also dirt farmers with 40 acres and a mule. It was where the blues were born. Jazz came up river from New Orleans. In the small black churches, in the small white churches, and in the Saturday night honky-tonk, Elvis blended gospel, blues, and jazz to create rock 'n roll music that captured the kids of the '50s and '60s.

Growing up on the Arkansas side of the Mississippi inspired John Grisham to write about his childhood in *A Painted House*, his first major work outside the legal thriller genre.

CARSON COUNTY

McLean was first established as a cattle loading pen site on the Rock Island Railroad in 1900. An English rancher donated the range-land site.

Carson County includes Panhandle, White Deer, and Groom.

Early blooming lilacs surround the First Presbyterian Church of Pampa.

The center of community life in Carson County towns is the schools, and school spirit is alive and well in residents from eight to eighty.

The Panhandle provides an extraordinary academic background for its residents, allowing them to compete with graduates from much more cosmopolitan areas. For crops, "cotton is king;" but really, "education is king." Ninety percent of Panhandle ranchers and farmers hold college degrees.

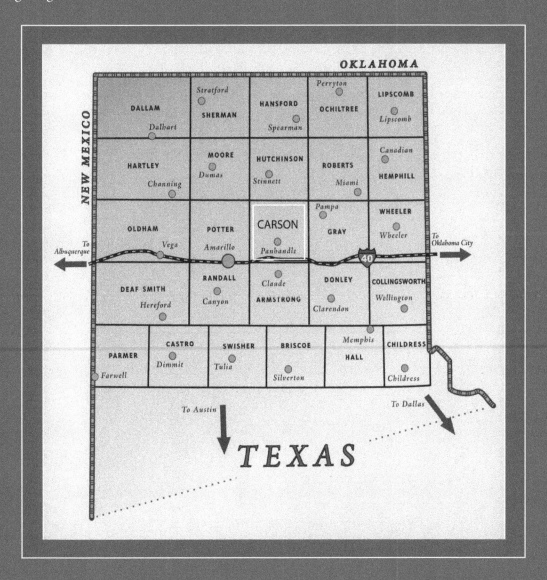

"Oklahoma!" soundtrack:
OOOOk-lahoma, where the wind comes sweepin' down the plain,
And the wavin' wheat can sure smell sweet,
When the wind comes right behind the rain.
OOOOk-lahoma, Ev'ry night my honey lamb and I,
Sit alone and talk and watch a hawk makin' lazy circles in the sky.
We know we belong to the land
And the land we belong to is grand!
And when we say
Yeeow! Aye-yip-aye-yo-ee-ay!
We're only sayin'
You're doin' fine, Oklahoma!
Oklahoma O.K.!

Old Route 66 can be traced back to the main route of the Ozark Trail that had markers along the rail. Route 66 came down from Chicago through Missouri and Oklahoma.

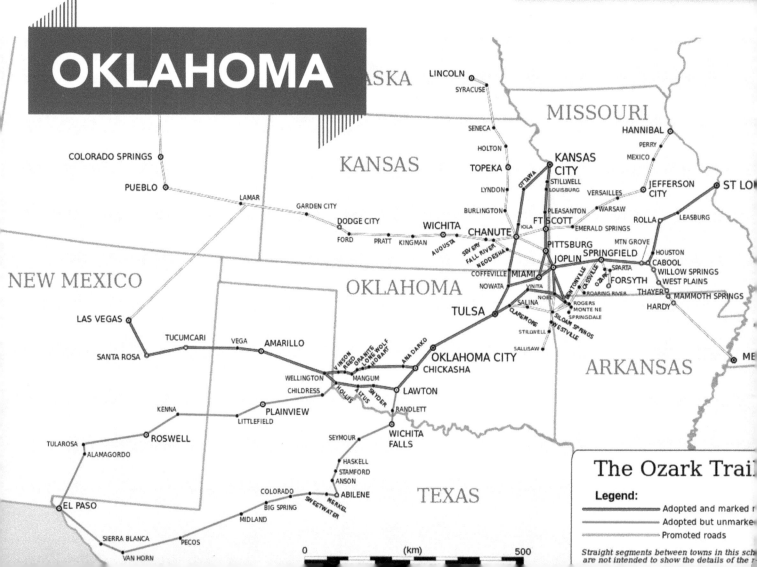

OKLAHOMA

The Ozark Trail

Legend:

—— Adopted and marked r

—— Adopted but unmarke

⋯⋯ Promoted roads

Straight segments between towns in this sch are not intended to show the details of the r

0   (km)   500

GEORGE WASHINGTON CARVER OF MISSOURI

His contribution to productivity helped the poor farmers grow crops for their own food and earn income to improve their quality of life.

He was hailed as, "One of America's great scientists," during World War II, and was recruited to join Tuskegee's College in Alabama, the same school from which came "Tuskegee Airmen," who flew fighter planes who escorted American bombers out of Britain in the War of Europe.

DALLAS METRO MAP

Dallas has more green space than any other city in America.

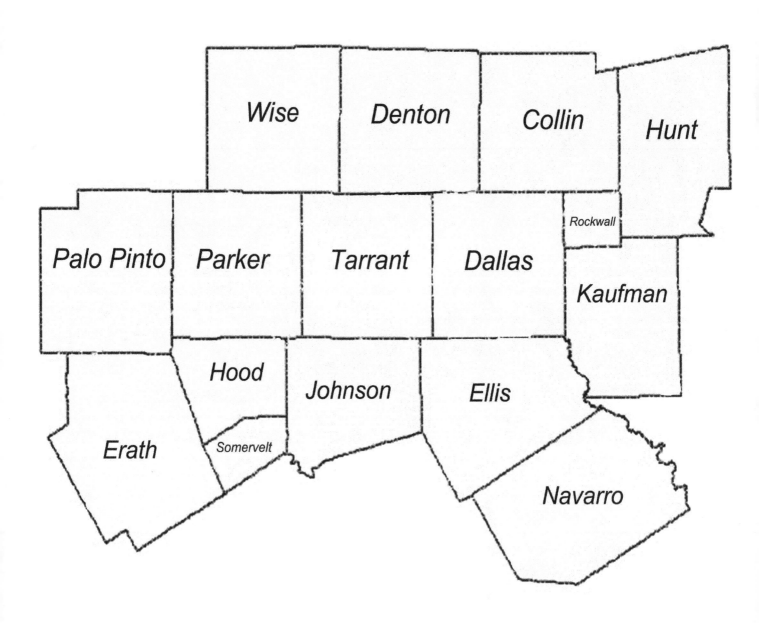

ABOUT THE FAMILY

Sam Wyly

Sam Wyly was raised in small-town Louisiana and got his MBA from the University of Michigan. His road to Dallas was by plane from Monroe to Shreveport to Tyler to Love Field. He began his career as a salesman for IBM. At 28, he created his first company, University Computing Company, the first of six enterprises Wyly grew to over $1 billion valuations. Over the next fifty years, he became one of America's top entrepreneurs, building companies in industries ranging from oil and gold mining to arts and crafts, from software to budget steakhouses and clean electricity. Wyly resides in Dallas, is a Christian Scientist, and has six children, twelve grandchildren, and seven great-grandchildren. He is an American entrepreneur and businessman, father, author, philanthropist, and major contributor to conservative campaigns and candidates. Wyly is the author of *Texas Got it Right!, 1,000 Dollars & An Idea: Entrepreneur to Billionaire,* and *The Immigrant Spirit: How Newcomers Enrich America.* An avid reader and great advocate of learning, his greatest legacy are his children.

Laurie Matthews

Laurie Matthews was born and raised in Dallas. She is a life-long member of The First Church of Christ, Scientist. She has enjoyed the fruits of the concept, "All Roads Lead to Dallas," because it brought her true love and husband David into her life from Oklahoma City. After graduating from Principia College in Elsah, Illinois, she taught English to children in Kaohsiung, Taiwan. Next, Laurie explored following in her father's footsteps by working in the customer service department of a software company. In raising their three grown children, Laurie was an active volunteer in their Montessori school and has been president of its board. She is active in her church, serving as clerk and reading room librarian. She and her twin sister Lisa were soccer teammates in Highland Park and at Principia College.

Andrew Wyly

Andrew Wyly is an entrepreneur, investor, and film producer. Born and raised in Malibu Colony, with some schooling in the Santa Monica Mountains in California and at the American school in Switzerland, he has been a Texan by choice since 2004. After earning a bachelor's degree in history from Denison University, Andrew worked as a sales agent for Green Mountain Energy and managed a portfolio for a hedge fund. He has continued his interest in political economics through participation with several think tanks and with his dad at the Philadelphia Convention that nominated George W. Bush for president. In 2007, he created the Andrew Wyly Film Company. *Blood Shot* was his first feature film.

Evan Wyly

Evan Wyly was born and raised in Dallas. After Highland Park High School he studied Economics at Princeton University and earned an MBA from Harvard Business School. He is a founder of Maverick Capital, Green Mountain Energy, and The Texas Legends. Previously, he was a director of three publicly traded companies: Sterling Software, Sterling Commerce, and Michaels Stores. He is active in his church, Young Presidents' Organization, and on the board of the Maverick Capital Foundation. He is married and has 3 children and 7 grandchildren.

Christiana Wyly

Christiana Wyly curates and catalyzes conversations on the future of food through research, events and advocacy. She also curates the Flourish content for the Near Future Summit and is completing a Food Policy dissertation on the future of meat at City University London. Previously, she was the Executive Director of Food Choice Taskforce, a focused research policy initiative on sustainable diets. Since 2008 she has been an operating partner at Satori Capital, an investment firm focused on sustainable investing, providing conscious capital,

and helping to grow the market for products and firms dedicated to a sustainable future. She was a founding partner of Zaadz.com, an online network for people who want to change the world, which was sold in 2007. She lives in Boulder, Colorado.

Lisa Wyly

Lisa Wyly is a professional sign language interpreter living in Texas with her husband and two children. Lisa's immersion into the Deaf community and American Sign Language began when she lost her hearing in early adulthood. With prayer and her family's loving support, Lisa embraced this challenge. Deaf Action Center in Dallas, TX, provided her with support services assisting her in coping with hearing loss. Lisa's parents and siblings learned sign language. Lisa received her master's degree in Deaf Education at Boston University. She remained in Boston joyfully living and working within the Deaf community. Fifteen years after losing her hearing, Lisa was healed of profound deafness. Today, she is grateful to be serving on the board of Deaf Action Center. Lisa loves spending time with family, enjoys

volunteering at her children's schools, and watching Monday night football with her dad. Her family still loves her even though she's a Boston Patriots fan.

Kelly Wyly O'Donovan

Kelly Wyly O'Donovan was born and raised in Dallas. After studies at Lewis & Clark College and Southern Methodist University with an art focus, she started a custom ceramics business, Wyly Works, Inc. Following additional art studies in France, she subsequently opened Elliott Yeary Gallery Fine Art & Jewelry in Dallas with her childhood friend, Kristin (née Schroeder) Yeary. Elliott Yeary Gallery, now located in Aspen, Colorado, has been in operation for over 20 years. She is a founding partner with her husband, Denis Finbarr O'Donovan, at Finbarr's Irish Pub & Kitchen. Kelly is an active volunteer and is involved in supporting multiple charitable organizations benefitting children and the environment. Kelly currently works as

a professional artist and exhibits in her Aspen gallery. She is mother to three wonderful sons.

Photo Credits

Please note that all photos, graphics and maps are Courtesy of Sam Wyly unless otherwise noted, and that every attempt has been made to credit the appropriate owners of these images.

9 - Covered wagon, pioneer kitchen, and kettle on campfire – Courtesy of Dreamstime Stock Photos

10-11 – David Wright/Courtesy of the Wyly Family

12-13 – Longhorn cattle Courtesy of Dreamstime Stock Photos

14 – King Cotton Photo Courtesy of Dreamstime Stock Photos

15 –Cotton boll, harvested cotton, and Mansion on Turtle Creek Courtesy of Dreamstime Stock Photos

16 – Natchitoches book cover Courtesy of Arcadia Publishing

17 – Photo Courtesy of Alfred Membreno

18 – Carriage to Enrico Caruso Opera 1908; Algorithm Map Courtesy of Dash Nelson-Rae of Plos One 2016

19 –Railroad Courtesy of Dreamstime Stock Photos

20 - Model T Courtesy of Dreamstime Stock Photos

21 – Wedding Photo Courtesy of Evan Wyly

22 – Alamo Photos Courtesy of Dreamstime Stock Photos

23 – Lisa Wyly Courtesy of Lisa Wyly; Andrew Wyly Courtesy of Andrew Wyly; Neely Cabin Courtesy of Alamy Stock Photo

25 – Methodist Church and teacher, Hattie Dyer, Photos Courtesy of Krum Historical Society; Classroom Courtesy of Dreamstime Stock Photos; Images of Krum book cover Courtesy of Arcadia Publishing

28 – "Boom Town" movie poster Courtesy of Alamy Stock Photo

29 – Route 66 in Texas book cover Courtesy of Arcadia Publishing; Magnolia gas station Courtesy of Dreamstime Stock Photos; Route 66 sign Courtesy of Dreamstime Stock Photos; Route 66 Highway Courtesy of Dreamstime Stock Photos

30 – Bridge photo Courtesy of Dreamstime Stock Photos

31 – Bridge photo Courtesy of Dreamstime Stock Photos

32-33 – Margaret Hunt Hill Bridge Courtesy of Dreamstime Stock Photos

34 – David Wright/Courtesy of the Wyly Family

35 –Paintings-David Wright/Courtesy of the Wyly Family

36 – Paper Mill Courtesy of Dreamstime Stock Photos

37 – Horse Jumping and Rex Tillerson Photos Courtesy of Dreamstime Stock Photos

38 – Highway 80 photo Courtesy of SVarner for American Roads; Don Henley Courtesy of Dreamstime Stock Photos; Lady Bird Johnson Courtesy of Aaron Shikler [Public domain], via Wikimedia Commons

39 – Photo Courtesy of Dreamstime Stock Photos

40 –Western Union Courtesy of Courtesy of Dreamstime Stock Photos

41 – Tractor Courtesy of Dreamstime Stock Photos

43 –Rex Tillerson Courtesy of Dreamstime Stock Photos

44 – Stagecoach Courtesy of Denver Public Library/Western History Collection

45 – Louisiana Bayou Courtesy of Dreamstime Stock Photos; Dr. Pepper can Courtesy of Dreamstime Stock Photos

46 – Comanche Woman Photo Courtesy of Dreamstime Stock Photos

48 – Juarez School Courtesy of Dallas Historical Society/The Dallas Morning News; Dallas's Little Mexico book cover Courtesy of Arcadia Publishing

54 – HP High School Grad Photos Courtesy of The Dallas Morning News; Clayton Twins Photo Courtesy of George Clayton

55 – Texas A&M Photo Courtesy of Dreamstime Stock Photos

58 – Scott Joplin Image Courtesy of Dreamstime Stock Photos

59 – Photos of Musicians Courtesy of Dreamstime Stock Photos

62 – Stephan Pyles Photo by Ron Ruggless; Stephan Pyles Flora Street Cafe Photos Courtesy of Dreamstime Stock Photos

66 – Windmill and Wind Turbine Photos Courtesy of Dreamstime Stock Photos

67 – Clint Murchison Sr. Photo Courtesy of Murchison Capital Partners

68 – Pegasus Photo Courtesy of Dreamstime Stock Photos

69 – Pegasus Magnolia Building Photo Courtesy of Bud Biggs Collection, Texas/Dallas History and Archives Division, Dallas Public Library. PA84-9/212

70 –IBM Logo Courtesy of Dreamstime Stock Photos

71 – Granddaddy H.L. Hunt Photo Courtesy of Hunt Oil Company

74 – Microchip Photo Courtesy of Dreamstime Stock Photos

76 – Underwood Typewriter Photo Courtesy of Dreamstime Stock Photos; iPhone Photo Courtesy of Dreamstime Stock Photos

77 – Steve Wolens and Laura Miller Photo Courtesy of Steve Wolens

78 – Texas Grid Graph Courtesy of Electric Reliability Council of Texas, Wind Technologies Market Report, Lawrence Berkeley National Laboratory, Texas Commission on Environmental Quality

79 – Burger Photo Courtesy of Dreamstime Stock Photos

81 – Graph Courtesy of U.S. Census Data

82 – Photo Courtesy of Remmzo

83 – Braniff Photos Courtesy of Dallas Historical Society

84 – American Airlines' Photo Courtesy of Dreamstime Stock Photos

85 – Mark Cuban Photo Courtesy of Alamy Stock Photo

86 – Federal Reserve Bank Photo-1930s

87 – "A Good Place for Seniors" Photos Courtesy of Dreamstime Stock Photos; Couple in Circle Photo Courtesy of Gab Goncalves

88 – Edgemere Photo Courtesy of The Edgemere; Trailer Park Photo Courtesy of Dreamstime Stock Photos

89 – Texas Ranger Badge Photo Courtesy of Dreamstime Stock Photos ; Frank Hamer Statue Photo Courtesy of Dreamstime Stock Photos

90 – Big Inch Little Inch Pipeline Photo-1942; FDR Photo Courtesy of Margaret Suckley-1941

91 – Dorie Miller Photo Courtesy U.S. Federal Government Public Domain; Sam Dealey Photo Courtesy of U.S. Federal Government Public Domain; WASP Photo Courtesy of ABC News-1943; Audie Murphy Photo Courtesy of U.S. Federal Government Public Domain

93 – Three Military Muscle Aircraft Photos Courtesy of Dreamstime Stock Photos

94 – "Howdy, Friend" Poster-1945

95 – New Orleans' Shipyard Photo Courtesy of public domain

96 –Soldiers' Arrival with Boy Scouts Photo Courtesy of Dreamstime Stock Photos

97 – Wedding Photo of General Eisenhower and Mamie Doud-1916

99 – Thanksgiving Square Photo Courtesy of Dreamstime Stock Photos

100 – Thanksgiving Square Mosaic Photo Courtesy of Evan Wyly

101 – St. Patrick's Cathedral in Fort Worth Photo Courtesy of Farragutful on Wikipedia Commons

102 – Church Photos Courtesy of Laurie Matthews

104 – U.S. Navy USS George H. W. Bush Carrier (CVN 77) Courtesy of U.S. Federal Government Public Domain; George H. W. Bush Naval Photo & George Bush Presidential Library Photos Courtesy of George Bush Presidential Library

106 – George P. Bush Photo Courtesy of Gage Skidmore

108-109 – Jerry Jones and Family Photo Courtesy of John Glaser; AT&T Stadium Courtesy of Dreamstime Stock Photos

111 – Dallas Texans' Helmet Photo Courtesy of Ryan Petkoff

112 –Pitcher Clayton Kershaw Photo Courtesy of Dreamstime Stock Photos

113 – Frisco, Texas Water Tower Courtesy of Laurie Matthews

114 – Texas Legends Basketball Photos Courtesy of Malcolm K. Farmer; Dr. Pepper Ballpark in Frisco, Texas Courtesy of Rainchill-Creative Commons Attribution

115 – Mr. & Mrs. Dirk Nowitzki Photo Courtesy of Dreamstime Stock Photos ; Karl Malone Basketball Photo Courtesy Dreamstime Stock PhotosPage 116 – Golfer Jordan Spieth Photo Courtesy of Dreamstime Stock Photos; Golfer Lee Trevino Photo Courtesy of Dreamstime Stock Photos

117 – Toddie Lee Wynne's Star Brand Ranch Photos Courtesy of Dreamstime Stock Photos

118 – Dallas City Councilwoman Photos of Mrs. Anita Martinez Courtesy of Anita N. Martinez Archive

119 – Lucchese Boots Photo Courtesy of Lucchese Boot Company

120 –Scouts' Oath Photo Courtesy of Dreamstime Stock Photos

121 – Highland Park Pharmacy Photo Courtesy of The Dallas Morning News

122 – Cheryl & Sam Wyly Animal Shelter Photos Courtesy of Seth Sachson

123 – Fort Worth Live Stock Exchange Photo Courtesy of Dreamstime Stock Photos ; Stock Show Photos Courtesy of Dreamstime Stock Photos

124 – President John F. Kennedy Outside Movie Theater Courtesy of Getty Images

125 – Allie Beth Allman Photo Courtesy of Allie Beth Allman

126 – Possum Kingdom Photo Taken by Mark and Hendley Quadling

127 – Karen Hughes Photo Courtesy of Wiki Commons

129 – Rick Perry Photo Courtesy of Wiki Commons

131 – Governor Greg Abbott Photo Courtesy of Wiki Commons

132 – Bonnie & Clyde Photo-1933

133 – Cokesbury Bookstore Photo-1925

134 – Elvis Presley Postage Stamp Photo Courtesy of Dreamstime Stock Photos

136 – Ozark Trail Obelisk Courtesy of Dreamstime Stock Photos

137 – George Washington Carver Photo Courtesy of Dreamstime Stock Photos

140-143 – Marc Klionsky/Courtesy of the Wyly Family

Back Cover Photo Courtesy of Michael Ainsworth

www.ingramcontent.com/pod-product-compliance
Lightning Source LLC
Jackson TN
JSHW071955131224
75386JS00050B/1787